# The No-Fluff Freelance Writing Pack Mega Workbook

By Alina Bradford

Alinabradford.com

No part of this course may be reproduced without the consent of the author.

# Table of Contents

4

# Introduction

When I read an article, book chapter, or blog post that gives me a great piece of information I literally get a warm glowy feeling in my midsection. Honestly. Typically, though, to get to those awesome morsels you have to wade through a bog of personal stories or build-up. I'm too impatient at least 83.682% of the time and just skim the yada-yada to get to the nugget.

So, I am going to do for you what I wish most writers would do: I'm going to get to the point. In this book, you will find nothing but awesome, actionable nuggets that you can use to build your own freelance business.

Hey, looks! Even this introduction is short.

You're welcome.

# Backstory

Feel free to totally skip this section if you want, but I figured that I would break down my qualifications for writing this course. I imagine if you bought the course, you already know, but I'll put it here, just in case.

I have been a freelance writer for almost two decades. That's a long f-ing time, yall. My LinkedIn profile boasts big clients like CBS, MTV, eBay, Zappos and a smattering of other impressive names. Those impressive names came from a LOT of mistakes. That's kind-of why I wanted to write this course. I want to help others that have a hunger to write make good money without all the stumbles I made.

As a teenager, I had heard someone (I think it was Oprah) say that you need to pick a career that you enjoy and that's easy for you. The thing I was best at was researching and writing. What job has that? Journalism!

So, I created my neighborhood's first weekly newspaper while I was in high school and encouraged the local kids to participate. It was a lot of fun and great practice.

Then -- after my counselor begged me to reconsider and tried to convince me that there's no money in writing-- I went to journalism school, became the editor of the college newspaper, won the very first Journalism Student of the Year award and ended up a few credits short of a diploma. Yah, that's a long story for another time.

I went on to write and edit for local non-profits to ramp up my clippings for my portfolio and tried to get jobs at local newspapers and magazines. My lack of diploma wasn't impressive, though, no matter how many great clips I had.

Something wonderful happened at that point. I was screwing around on the internet in an AOL chatroom and saw an ad for an online weekly writing competition with monetary prizes. At that moment, something clicked. I could make money writing online from my home! I didn't have to write for newspapers to make money!

From there I wrote for whoever would pay me. This wasn't the brightest thing I did in my career. I took jobs paying $10 an article and typed my fingers to the bone every day. I had kids to feed and rent to pay, so I did it.

Eventually, to no surprise, I got tired of it. My brain felt like a fried egg cooked by one of those people Gordon Ramsey yells at on his reality shows. "This egg is so overdone it looks like you cooked it in hellfire and then blasted it into the sun, you cow!"

I needed higher paying clients, so I didn't need to work as much. It took some time, but I did it. Here's how I got there, and you can, too.

# What You Need for This Course

I hate courses that you pay good money for and then realize you need to buy a crapton of extra stuff to complete the course.

This isn't like that.

All you need to complete my course is an internet connection, a computer, a pen and a notebook. I'm pretty sure you already have those, so you're all set.

I'm serious about using the notebook, by the way. Grab a fresh notebook and write "My Freelancing Notebook" on the front. Use it only for working on your freelance business.

Write down every answer to every question in this course. Brainstorm your answers on the notebook pages. Write everything out. It may seem silly but writing things out instead of ticking them off in your head will get your creative juices flowing and help you come up with better ideas.

You want your freelance writing business to be awesome? Write it out.

# Chapter 1: How to Write a Paragraph the Right Way

Let's start out with the basics. Writing a paragraph is one of the simplest parts of writing.

No doubt you can write a sentence, that's easy. The problem comes when you try to lace those sentences together to make a paragraph, and then go on to write another paragraph.

No matter if you're just starting out as a writer, or have some experience under your belt, this chapter will get your work read and published. Sit back and take notes.

## The First Line

There are several types of paragraphs. The type of paragraph you're writing determines what your opening sentence will be. Types of paragraphs include:

An introduction paragraph- These are found at the beginning of a blog or article and are meant to draw the reader in while giving them a pretty firm idea of what the rest of the paragraphs are about.

Think of it as a hey-I've-got-something-awesome-for-you-so-here's-a-little-summary paragraph. Hit them with an interesting fact or statistic. Try to get this done in three to four sentences. Be sure to use your keyword as soon as possible, too.

Example:

"40 percent of writers don't know how to write a paragraph correctly, according to Writing XYZ Magazine. That's a shocking statistic, but you may be in that percentage and not even know it. Here's what you need to know so that you're not part of the clueless masses."

Standard paragraph- The first line of a standard paragraph is meant to either introduce the reader to a topic or to continue a thought from the last paragraph.

Closing paragraph- A closing paragraph sums up what your post was about and tells the reader what to do next. This can be encouraging the reader to click on a link to an article, book, item you're selling, whatever. No matter what you guide your reader to next, this bit is called a Call to Action (CTA).

# Inside the Paragraph

Once you have the opening sentence down, there are a few rules you need to follow.

First, don't repeat the main word in every line. For example:

Wrong: "40 percent of writers don't know how to write a paragraph correctly, according to Writing XYZ Magazine. That's a shocking statistic about writers, but you may be in that percentage and not even know it. Here's what you need to know so that you're not part of the clueless writer's club."

Notice I used the word "writers" in every sentence. That's bad. Not only does it make the paragraph boring, writing the same word over and over again will hurt the article's SEO (we'll talk more about SEO later). Break out your thesaurus and use synonyms when you can.

For example, here's some words that can replace writer in the sample paragraph:

➤ Word wranglers

➤ Scribes

➤ Author, journalist, poet, blogger, columnist (depending on what type of writer you're talking about)

Next, be sure that each sentence is different. Using sentences that are the same length is boring. Mix it up.

Use:

➤ A short sentence

➤ A compound sentence (a sentence that uses 'and,' 'or,' 'but,' 'though,' a semicolon or a colon, etc.)

➤ A sentence that uses a comma

➤ Quotes

➤ Statistics

You get the idea. Sentence salad. Just make sure that each sentence makes sense in how it connects to the sentence before it. Using different lengths of sentences, but not making them work together in a harmonious stream of thought isn't going to work.

Check out the difference between these two paragraphs:

Writing is fun. It takes work. Keep being creative. Use variety. Keep readers entertained.

Writing is fun, but it takes work. Keep being creative. Use variety to keep readers entertained.

Thought the first paragraph is perfectly fine, it's boring and choppy because it only used super short sentences. Mixing up the sentence structures made the paragraph more interesting.

Finally, be sure to always transition from one paragraph to the next. You can do this by using transitional words in the first sentence. These words continue the thought from the last paragraph.

Some transitional words and phrases include:

➢ 'First,' 'second,' and 'third'
➢ Next
➢ Finally
➢ Again
➢ Also
➢ Then
➢ Though
➢ Additionally
➢ On the other hand
➢ Remember
➢ Don't forget
➢ Conversely
➢ Even though
➢ Not only
➢ Actually
➢ Besides
➢ Likewise
➢ Hence
➢ Thus

- ➢ Later
- ➢ Immediately
- ➢ Meanwhile
- ➢ Therefore
- ➢ Consequently
- ➢ For instance
- ➢ For example
- ➢ Of course
- ➢ Otherwise
- ➢ Still
- ➢ Yet
- ➢ In contrast

Take a look back at my previous paragraphs in this chapter and you'll see I use transitional words a lot. They help your reader follow your thought process. Transitional words are particularly useful for guiding readers through how-to instructions.

# Bullet Points and Numbered Lists

A great way to make your work easy to read is by breaking paragraphs down into numbered or bulleted lists. There are some rules about using these lists properly, though.

First, use numbered lists when you're explaining steps of a how-to or project to your reader. Also, make sure you don't start each step start with a transition word. Your numbers are doing that for you.

Right:

1. Pour the batter into the bowl.

2. Add ½ cup of milk.

3. Stir until the batter starts to bubble.


Wrong:

1. First, pour the batter into the bowl.

2. Next, add ½ cup of milk.

3. Finally, stir until the batter starts to bubble.

Use bulleted lists when you have a list of items or points. For example, say I was writing an article about monkeys and wanted to make a list of foods they like to eat. My bulleted list would look something like this:

- Fruits

- Nuts

- Seeds

- Flowers

Notice that in the numbered list I used punctuation and in the bulleted list I did not? The rule is that if you're writing a full sentence, use punctuation in your list. If you are just listing an item, skip the punctuation.

The first word in your numbered or bulleted lists must always be capitalized, though. There's no budging on that one.

Pro tip: Make sure your lists don't start with the same word. Mix it up.

Right:

- Click the right button.
- Scroll to the Start menu and select it.
- Choose the program from the list.

Wrong:

- Click the right button.
- Click the Start menu.
- Click on the program from the list.

# Get Your Paragraph's Spelling and Grammar Right

Top-notch writing skills are a necessity to make a living as a writer, of course. The English language is tricky business, however, and remembering all the rules can be hard.

Never fear!

This list of dozens of easy-to-remember tricks will help you improve your spelling and grammar, giving your writing skills the polish they need.

## Passive or Active Voice

Do you have a hard time figuring out the difference between passive and active voice? Try this trick: Add the phrase "by zombies" to the end. If it still makes sense, it's passive voice. So "She was carried away" is passive, because "She was carried away by zombies" would make sense.

## What's a Preposition?

Not sure what a preposition is? It's anything a squirrel can do to a tree: it can go up a tree, it can go down a tree, it can go in a tree or out a tree or around a tree... All those words—up, down, in, out, around—are prepositions.

## Sit vs. Set vs. Lay vs. Lie

Sit, set, lay and lie are confused a lot. Basically, sit and lie are used when someone is getting comfortable. They both have an "I" so use that to remember that they are used for a person or some type of living being. For example, you tell a child to sit, not set.

Set and lay are used when something is being placed somewhere. They both need an object in the sentence. For example, "I set my glass down on the table."

## Desert or Dessert?

A desert is a dry, arid plot of land, while dessert is a delicious morsel of food often enjoyed after dinner. If you struggle to keep the two separated in your head, just remember this: Dessert has 2 Ss because you want more and more of it.

## Principle or Principal?

A principle is a basis for a belief in something, while a principal is the head of a school. The old rule is just to remember your principal is your pal.

# How Do You Spell Cemetery?

Struggling to remember how to spell cemetery? Remember that it has 3 Es—like in the word Eeek!

# My Brother and I or My Brother and Me

My brother and I went to the store together—or was it my brother and me? If you're pairing yourself with another person and aren't sure which to say, take the other person out first.

You would never say "Me went to the store"—you'd say "I went to the store"—so in that case, it would be "My brother and I." On the other hand, you would say "She let me borrow her car," so for that one, it would be "She let my brother and me borrow her car."

# Coordinating Conjunctions

Coordinating conjunctions are words that can be used after commas to link two independent clauses together. To remember your coordinating conjunctions, just remember the acronym FANBOYS: For And Nor But Or Yet So.

# Decimate Defined

Most people think the word "decimate" means to completely destroy something. The key to the actual definition lies in the root word—"deci"—like "decimal" or "decibel." Decimate, by definition, actually means to reduce something by one tenth.

## Less or Fewer

Not sure when to use less or fewer? Less is when you're talking about something not quantifiable by a number, while fewer is used when you're talking about something you could count. So, for example, grocery store signs should say, "14 items or fewer," not "14 items or less," because you can count how many items in your cart.

Note that the distinction between less and fewer is if you can count something, not if you would want to count something. So you would say, "I would like the beach to have less sand," or you could say, "I would like the beach to have fewer grains of sand"—because while you wouldn't count all the grains of sand at the beach, grains of sand are something that can be counted, while sand, on its own, is not.

# Do or Make

Do you do housework or make housework? Of the two, "do" is an active verb, so here's the test you use:  Does it feel like work? If the answer is yes, you use the word "do." Otherwise, you use the word "make."

So, you would do housework, but you would make friends. Another test is creation. If you're creating something, use make. If you're doing something, use do.

# Adjectives vs. Adverbs

Adjectives and adverbs are both description words. The difference between the two? Adjectives describe nouns while adverbs describe verbs. One easy trick to remember is that adverbs often end in "ly"—like quickly or stealthily— while most of your other description words, like purple or sly, are adjectives.

# Good vs. Well

When someone asks how you are, do you say, "I'm doing good" or do you say, "I'm doing well?" Believe it or not, there's a difference. The word "good" has a moral basis to it, whereas the word "well" has to do with how you're feeling.

So, if you say, "I'm doing good," what you're actually saying is that you're doing something morally good—charity work, for example—whereas if you say you're doing well, you mean you're not ailing in any way.

# Misplaced Modifiers

Modifiers should always go next to the subject they're modifying, but we misplace them in language all the time. When you're trying to check your writing for this, just remember that mechanics don't leak oil.

What does that mean? Consider the following sentence: "Leaking oil, the mechanic fixed the car."

What that sentence is saying is that the mechanic is leaking oil, though clearly it should be the car that is leaking oil. So, it should read: "Leaking oil, the car was fixed by the mechanic."

## Always Compare Apples to Apples

Have you heard the phrase "comparing apples to oranges?" What this means is that you need to make sure that when you are comparing two items, they're actually equivalent.

Consider this sentence: The novels of Ernest Hemingway are shorter than William Faulkner. This is comparing Ernest Hemingway's novels to William Faulkner, not to William Faulkner's novels.

When comparing items in a sentence, you may need to make the sentence longer to be sure you're comparing apples to apples. The sentence above, for example, should read, "The novels of Ernest Hemingway are shorter than the novels of William Faulkner," to avoid confusion.

## Affect vs. Effect

Struggling to remember the difference between affect and effect? Just remember that A is for action. Affect is a verb form of influence and means "to have an impact on."

For example, you would say "Do you think the weather will affect the turn-out at tomorrow's cook out?"

Effect, on the other hand, is the result of an action. For example, you would say "His new airbrushing technique gave his work a cool effect."

## What Are Transitions?

Transitions are words that lead you from one idea to the next. They literally make a transition. You need these words to guide your reader from one word to the next.

## Its vs. It's

Can't keep its and it's straight? Just remember that it's is longer because it's really two words: It is. So, if you can replace the word with "it is", then you need the version with the apostrophe. If not, it is the word to us.

## Then vs. Than

Then versus than is easy to remember when you keep in mind that then has an E because it describes eons of time. For example, "I liked being a kid; things were easier back then."

Than, on the other hand, is a comparison word. For example, "This tree is smaller than your tree."

## I.e. vs. E.g.

I.E. and E.G. are both abbreviations of Latin words, and once you know what they're abbreviations of, it's much easier to use them correctly. I.e. stands for "Id Est" which means "In other words."

It's used when restating an idea, usually as a way to simplify it. e.g. stands for "Exempli Gratia" and means "For example."

# I Before E

We've all heard the phrase "I before E except after C," but sometimes we forget that there's a second part to this rhyme. The full rhyme is "I before E except after C, or in sounding as 'A' as in Neighbor or Weigh." And don't forget, the word "weird" is weird.

## Stationery vs. Stationary

If you mix these two words up, just remember that "E" is for "Envelopes" while "A" is for "Automobiles." So, if you're talking about the paper you'd stick in an envelope, it's stationery. If you're talking about being stuck in your car and not moving, you're stationary.

## How to Spell Because

Struggling to spell because? Remember this mnemonic device:

"Big Elephants Always Upset Small Elephants."

## How to Spell Necessary

Sometimes it's hard to remember if necessary has one C and 2 Ss or 2 Cs and one S. A helpful way to remember is you can have one collar and two socks.

## Practice vs. Practise

Mixing up these two words? Remember that practise is a verb with an "S" for "sport," while practice with a "C" is the noun.

## How to Spell Rhythm

Trying to remember how to spell rhythm? Remember this mnemonic device: "Rhythm helps your two hips move."

## How to Spell Island

When you're remembering how to spell island, remember than an island is land with water all around.

## Piece vs. Peace

Mixing up piece and peace? Just remember that you want a piece of pie.

## Lose vs. Loose

Lose is to misplace, so it misplaced an O. Loose, on the other hand, is not too tight, so it has room for an extra O.

## What's a Semicolon?

Despite its name, a semicolon shouldn't be used to replace a colon. In fact, it's used to replace a period, separating two closely related sentences.

## Quotations

Here's a quick and easy rule about quotations: Punctuation always stays inside. So even if you're ending a sentence with a quote, the period would go on the inside of the quotation marks, not the outside.

The only exception is when you have a quote inside of a sentence that ends with and question mark and the quote doesn't. For example: When someone asks how you are, do you say, "I'm doing good" or do you say, "I'm doing well"?

## Who vs. Whom

Not sure if you should use who or whom? Rephrase the statement as a question, and then answer it with either "he" or "him." If your answer is "he," then you want the word "who."

If your answer is "him," then you want the word "whom." E.g.: Matt is the one _____ we saw. Who did we see? We saw him.

So, it would be "Matt is the one whom we saw." Matt is the one _____ went first. Who went first? He did. So, it would be "Matt is the one who went first."

## That vs. Who/Whose/Whom

Not sure if you should use "that" or some form of "who?" That is an object word, while who is for people. If you remember that who is for who-mans (humans), you'll be using the words correctly.

## How to Spell Tomorrow

If you struggle to remember how to spell tomorrow, remember that it used to be two words: To and Morrow, as in, "Let's keep going to the morrow."

Over time, it was hyphenated into to-morrow, and finally combined to the form we know today — tomorrow.

## How to Spell Separate

The middle part of the word "separate" can be hard to keep track of. To remember it, remind yourself that an R separates two As.

# How to Spell Embarrass

It can be hard to keep track of how many Rs and Ss are in the word embarrass. The mnemonic device can help: "I get [R]eally [R]ed when my [S]ister [S]ings."

## How to Spell Horror

Think of the word "horror" as having two Os because you have to keep your eyes open in fear.

## How to Spell Special

Special is spelled with a CIA, because the CIA has Special Agents.

## Comma Usage

Here's a fun mnemonic to remember how to use commas: "A cat has claws at the end of its paws. A comma's a pause at the end of a clause."

## Double Negatives

Double negatives are not grammatically correct, and when you do use them, the two negatives end up countering each other, often saying the opposite of what you intended. Here's an easy saying to help you remember: "I don't know nothing about double negatives."

## What's an Interjection?

Here's a cute little poem to help you remember what an interjection is: "An interjection cries out, "Hark!" I need an exclamation mark!"

## How to Spell Exaggerate

To remember that exaggerate has two Gs, remember that "Goofy Greg loves to exaggerate."

## How to Spell Difficulty

Struggling to remember how to spell difficulty? Wrestle up some memories of the old Matilda movie and say to yourself what the kids said in that movie: Mrs. D, Mrs. I, Mrs. F. F. I., Mrs. C, Mrs. U, Mrs. L.T.Y.

## How to Spell Environment

Remember that a new environment will Iron Me out to get the middle letters in that word in the right order.

## How to Spell Truly

Because "truly" is spelled differently than its root word, true, it can be hard to remember how to spell it. Here's a little phrase that will remind you: "It is truly hot in July." Though they're pronounced differently, this can help you remember that truly and July are spelled similarly.

## Quite vs. Quiet

Can't remember which word you're trying to use? Remember this little phrase: "It is [Q]uite [U]nbelievably [I]mpossible [T]o [E]njoy Spelling Difficult Words."

## How to Spell Vacuum

When you're trying to remember how to spell "vacuum," remember the phrase "I See Two Ewes in the

Field." That will help you remember that there is 1 C and 2 Us.

## Compliment vs. Complement

Trying to remember the difference between compliment and complement? Remember that the opposite of a compliment is an insult, while when something complements something else, it enhances it in some way.

## Capital vs. Capitol

A capital, with an A, is a city where main government offices are. A capitol, with an O, is the building where laws are made. To remember the difference, remember that many capitols have domes, both of which have Os.

# Weather vs. Whether

Trying to remember whether to use the word weather or whether? Just remember: "In cold weather, you wear a sweater."

# Split Infinitives

An infinitive is the basic "to" form of a verb, like "to dance" or "to write." It's incorrect to split infinites.

Splitting infinitives is when you put a word between the "to" and the verb.

Keep in mind the opening line of Star Trek— "To boldly go where no man has gone before"—to remember. The line was mocked by Douglas Adams, who quipped, "To boldly split infinitives that no man had split before."

# How to Use Commas, Quotation Marks and Semicolons

Creating clean, mostly error-free content is important to freelance writers. Copy full of errors look unprofessional and can really turn off potential customers. You don't want to be lumped in with noobs! Edit!

Emails, blogs and social media encourage speed over accuracy, lulling many into the feeling that close is good enough.  If you plan on being a successful freelance writer, though, almost isn't good enough. Here are some tips to help you get closer to perfection.

## When to Use Commas

Get it right... or scare people away.

One of the most common problems even more skilled writers run into is how to use commas properly.

A comma is defined as a punctuation mark used to indicate the separation of ideas or elements or a pause in a sentence.

The biggest misuse of commas is often overuse. When in doubt, use a comma when there is an audible pause when you're saying the sentence out loud.

For example:

Jan, can you write the story, please?

This sentence has definite pauses when said aloud. Proper use of commas also keeps the meaning of a sentence clear.

For example:

Wrong - Jan loves to draw fish and write.

Jan likes to draw fish?

Right - Jan loves to draw, fish and write.

Notice that a comma wasn't used after the word "fish." It has become common to leave off the comma before "and" in a series, especially if you are writing for magazines or websites.

The last use of a comma is with a direct name or title.

For example:

The writer and artist, Jan, is my old friend.

Or

Would you draw me a picture, Jan?

Or

Jan Lang, Ph.D., is the author of some impressive articles.

# How to Mix Quotation Marks and Punctuation

Using punctuation with quotation marks isn't the mystery some think it is. In fact, there are only two major rules to remember:

Always use punctuation inside the quotation marks.

For example:

"The article is finished. It only took a week to do."

And

Jan said, "It only took a week."

Also, always use a comma before or after a quote is introduced.

For example:

Jan said, "The article is finished."

And

"The article is finished," cried Jan.

"Said" in the first sentence tells you that a quote is coming so it is followed by a comma.

In the second sentence, "cried Jan" tells you who just made the quote. In this case, there is a comma before "cried." Remember, the punctuation is always found inside the quotation marks.

## When to Use a Semicolon

Semicolons are an unloved punctuation, mostly because it is misunderstood. If used correctly, though, semicolons are an easy way to spice up a writer's prose, or at least show an editor that the writer is competent.

The rule to follow is: If there are two sentences that are complete thoughts and don't have a conjunction, you can use a semicolon to join them.

For example:

Jan's article is interesting; it is full of great quotes.

Sure, you could put a period between these two statements, but it sounds so much better with a semicolon. Basically, a semicolon shows a close relationship between two sentences and a pause just a little shorter than a period, but longer than a comma.

Now that your copy is treated with respect, romance will be on the way . Your customers will undoubtedly fall in love with the work and you can ride off into the sunset with a check in-hand.

# Get Rid of the Junk

There are a few clean-up tips you need to know to make your paragraphs easier to read and more interesting.

First, get rid of "that" whenever you can. If your sentence reads fine without it, toss it.

Next, declare war on "very." Very is a perfectly fine word, but it's boring. The word "very" is almost always unnecessary in your writing.

Mark Twain once said, "Substitute "damn" every time you're inclined to write very. Your editor will delete it and the writing will be just as it should."

Don't wait for the editor!

Here's some ways to mix things up. Change:

➢ "Very happy" to "jubilant" or "ecstatic"

➢ "Very eager" to "keen" or "excited"

- "Very painful" to "excruciating" or "agonizing"
- "Very weak" to "feeble" or "frail"
- "Very dry" to "parched" or "dehydrated"
- "Very poor" to "destitute" or "impoverished"
- "Very valuable" to "precious" or "prized"
- "Very neat" to "immaculate" or "tidy"
- "Very bright" to "dazzling" or "blinding"
- "Very hungry" to "starving" or "famished"
- "Very beautiful" to "exquisite" or "stunning"
- "Very strange" to "bizarre" or "unique"
- "Very serious" to "grave" or "solemn"
- "Very sleepy" to "exhausted" or "fatigued"

# Chapter 2: How to Make Your Writing Sound Formal or Informal

When you're taking jobs from clients, you'll notice that they will often ask for a "formal" or "casual" tone in your writing style. You need to have a good handle on what these styles are to please your clients. Here's how to make your writing fit with each one.

## Formal Style

When you see "formal" think business. It's basically how someone would speak to their CEO or upper management. There's typically:

No jokes

No contractions like don't, won't, can't, haven't

Industry terms

Third-person point-of-view only (don't use you, I, we, our)

Here's an example of formal writing:

*Blog Post: Strategies for Increasing Revenue in a Value-based Healthcare System*

*Combine Old Techniques with the New*

*The first step to creating a new revenue cycle that works with a value-based system is to combine the old with the new. The old methods of diagnosis and testing must be combined with new methods that provide a more holistic approach. This method will focus not just on a current ailment, but the patient's entire health and wellbeing as a whole. This for hospitals, this can include:*

*Providing better communication techniques*

*Incorporating better methods for reducing new infection during hospital stays and outpatient procedures*

*Reviewing and organizing data to get a clear view of the patient's overall health before making a diagnosis in the ER*

*Encouraging patients to participate in their care by enabling them to track their medical histories and other personal items easily through the hospital's website*

*Target New Demographics*

*To increase revenue, hospitals must create programs that will target patients who qualify for economic programs and are eligible for new funding sources in line with changes made by the Affordable Care Act (ACA) for increased revenue sustainability to compete with other hospitals in their area. Due to the ACA,*

Medicaid has been expanded to include an increased number of low-income adults. Some segments that are quickly growing are Dual Eligible and Hierarchical Condition Categories.

*Preparing Patient Financial Service to Properly Handle New Patients*

As part of increasing the patient experience, a provider's patient financial service must be able to help patients understand health insurance rules, co-pays, how networks function and plan options with patience and understanding. They also need to learn ways to guide the patient through the online Medicaid enrollment process and, if they are in eligible states, must learn the new guidelines for determining financial assistance through the ACA to better insure enhanced revenue cycle.

# Casual Style

Casual, friendly or informal style is basically how you'd talk to a friend. You would use second person or sometimes first person, and you would use slang, metaphors, jokes and contractions.

Just how casual you can be depends on the website. For example, if you were writing for the New York Times style section, your level of casualness would be a little more laced up than if you were writing for BuzzFeed.

Here's an example of a post written in a casual style:

***Blog Post: Why Syndication May be Your Best Content Solution***

*I recently did a poll of 129 business professionals on what their biggest problems were when it came to posting content to their website. A majority of those polled said that they didn't have time to post or that they couldn't find or write quality content that was fresh and/or innovative.*

*The results didn't surprise me.*

*Over the past 16 years I have heard these complaints time and time again. Business owners know that the key to getting more traffic to their site, and more customers, is posting great content search engines and visitors love. It's not an easy task to do when you are running a business, though.*

*There are usually two solutions.*

*One, the business owner can hire someone, like me, to create and post content on their site. Two, they can sign up at a syndication site to get pre-made content for their site. Today, I'm going to talk a little bit about syndication for those times when you can't hire someone like me.*

*You Get Fresh, Relevant Website Content*

*One of the benefits of getting content from a syndication service* is that the content is always fresh and relevant to your industry. One of the biggest complaints from the business owners I polled was that they can never come up with new ideas for articles and blog posts. All they can think of was the same old, tired ideas that their competitors have already covered.

With syndication, you get to pick from the latest articles to hit the web. Since it's unlikely that your competitor uses syndication, you will have the edge.

*You Get Quality Content*

Chances are, you probably aren't a writer or editor, so writing content yourself is out of the question, at least most of the time. Syndicated articles and blog posts come from the top digital publishers on the web. That means you are getting access to the best writers without the need to hire them. The content has also passed through the hands of some of the best editors on the web, which means the content will look professional, read well and *won't contain embarrassing spelling or grammar mistakes.*

*Get More Traffic*

*Now, I know what you're thinking. "Doesn't Google penalize sites that have duplicate content?" Yes, they do, but it is important to understand what Google considers duplicate content. The duplication rule only applies if you are posting the same article over and over again on one site (an early black hat SEO tactic). This rule doesn't pertain to an article posted on two different sites. So, no, you won't get penalized for using syndicated content that has already been published on another site.*

*Need proof? Ideal Media found that sites using their syndication service had an 83% increase in traffic. That doesn't sound like those sites are being penalized to me.*

*So, if you need fresh content, but don't want to create it yourself or hire others to do it for you, consider syndicated content. It*

*could be just what your site needs
to rise above your competitors.*

# Chapter 3: Everything Writers Need to Know About SEO

SEO is an abbreviation for search engine optimization, which, in a nutshell, means anything that helps a search engine find an article and rank it on the first page of search results. Go to Google and search for your favorite topic. See the first result? That article has excellent SEO.

So, how do you get these magical results? Well, only so much of it is in the hands of the writer. A lot of SEO has to do with the website's reputation. I'm going to cover what you, as a writer, needs to know about it to make your articles rank.

# Research Keywords

The first thing you do before you write an article is to research. Now, as an expert on your niche, you should have a pretty good idea about what people want to read. There's more to it than that, though. Keywords are a big way search engines know what your article is about and how to rank it in search.

To research keywords, go to Google Keyword Planner. Then, type in a word or phrase that describes what you want to write about.

A list of keywords will pop up. Look for keywords and phrases that have 10 to 100 thousand monthly searches. This means that people are actively typing these keywords into Google each month looking for articles on the topic. And in turn, Google actively searches for articles that provides information on these topics.

Another keyword search tool that's helpful is at https://app.neilpatel.com/en. It's super simple and free.

So, your articles should have keywords here and there throughout. Most of the time, keywords will naturally pop up in your writing. You don't really need to think about it too hard.

Just be sure that:

➢ You have a keyword in the title of the article or post and that it is close to the beginning

➢ There is a keyword in the name of the image files you use and in the captions

➢ Keywords are in the headings

➢ There is a least one keyword in the first or second sentence of the post

➢ DO NOT litter your article or post with keywords, though. Other than the areas I've highlighted, let them come naturally. If you spam an article with the same words over and over you'll get a penalty, which will make your post rank lower in searches.

# SEO-Friendly Headlines

Now you know that your posts should have keywords in the headings, but there is one more thing you should know. All of your headings should have H2 or H3 tags in the code.

Search engines look at your heading to figure out what your article is about. These tags help search engines know where your headings are.

Don't freak out!

You don't need to know coding. Most post editors and word processing software, like Word, have heading options.

Just highlight your heading, tap on the H2 or H3 heading option and you're golden. The tag will be automatically added to the code.

# Add Media

Search engines love when you use more than just text in your website content. Plus, media makes your content much more appealing to visitors, which is even more important. You don't want people to come to your posts, see nothing but boring text and click away!

The rule is to add at least two images to your post for good ranking, but the more the merrier. Some media you can add to a post are:

➢ Embedded videos

➢ Gifs

➢ Image galleries

➢ Audio recordings

➢ Videos of yourself explaining a concept

➢ Infographics

➢ Memes

➢ Surveys

> Maps

Think creating multimedia content takes too much time? Don't worry. There are plenty of websites out there that help you make your own GIFs, maps, charts, memes and more for free, in just a few minutes. There are also plenty of sites that let you use their multimedia content in your articles.

Try out a couple of these free tools. You'll be adding some snap to your content in no time.

## 1. PABLO

Have you ever lusted after those sites that have beautiful article images overlaid with pretty quotes or the titles of their articles? Well lust no more. Pablo by Buffer provides you with the beautiful stock images, the fonts and the layering capability. All you need to do is come up with the text.

## 2. BE FUNKY

I love Be Funky. You can use their tools to make your photos totally retro, in a good way. Groovy! They also have stock photos you can use for free.

### 3. PIC MONKEY

Pic Monkey is one of the most popular free photo editing software sites out there, and for good reason. Not only does it give you the capability to edit photos, you can also use it to create far out photo projects with overlays, frames, textures and more.

### 4. GIMP

When you need a huge amount of editing tools, but like a zero on the price tag, consider downloading GIMP. Think of GIMP as Photoshop's ugly twin. They both have tons of features, but GIMP is a little clunkier to use. Hey, the price is right, though!

### 5. MEME GENERATOR

Everyone is mad for memes and the Meme Generator makes creating your own simple and quick. Just browse through premade memes, add your own text, download them, and you're in business. Or, you can start from scratch with your own photo. Just upload your photo, fill in the text fields and boom! You've made your own meme.

## 6. EASEL.LY

Easel.ly is easily the most awesome visual tool I use. (See what I did there?) It gives you everything you need to create stunning infographics and simple drag-and-drop tools. I use it constantly for myself and my customers. The best part? Easel.ly creates code so that you can embed your infographic on websites.

The free version has a lot of great visuals to start with, but if you want to go pro, I recommend upgrading.

## 7. GIPHY

Sometimes you just need a snappy gif to make your blog post or social media post just a little more special. Never fear, Giphy is here to supply you will all the gifs your heart could possibly desire, for free.

## 8. THREE GRAPHS

Need a chart to illustrate some stats? Three Graphs is the site to hit up. You can create a variety of different types of charts, choose your chart's colors and more.

## 9. SIEGE MEDIA EMBEDDED CODE GENERATOR

How many times have you created an awesome visual and then wanted to allow people to share it, but remembered you don't know a thing about creating embedded code? I've been there! The solution is using Siege Media Embedded Code Generator. No skill required!

## 10. MAPBOX

Maps are a cool visual that's not utilized as often as it should be. MapBox makes creating your own maps easy and, dare I say it, fun. Just input your data and you're map comes out like you hired Magellan.

Here's a quick list of my 20 favorites (including the ones above) and what they do for easy reference:

> Giphy for GIFs

> Creative Commons for Creative Common photos

> YouTube for embeddable videos

> Easel.ly for infographics

> Meme Generator

> Pablo for quotes

> PhotoPin for Creative Commons photos

> DaFont for fonts

- ➢ Office Sway for presentations
- ➢ Pond5 for historic media files
- ➢ Survey Monkey for surveys
- ➢ NVD3 for charts
- ➢ Mapbox for maps
- ➢ OpenClipArt for clip art
- ➢ GetEmojis for emojis
- ➢ Pexels for modern, clean photos
- ➢ PhotoPin finds Creative Commons photos
- ➢ Pexel Videos for free stock videos
- ➢ ClipSafari for clipart
- ➢ MyEcoverMaker to create covers for ebooks
- ➢ Unsplash for free stock photos

# Quality Links Make SEO So Much Better

Finally, you need to add quality links in your articles. Link to reputable sites throughout your articles. Some reputable websites that search engines love are:

➢ Government sites like the FDA, National Library of Health, or the CDC

➢ Groups like the World Health Organization, American Dental Association or the American Cancer Society

➢ Science and health journals and magazines like JAMA and Scientific American

➢ Trusted health sites like the Mayo Clinic

➢ University websites

➢ Search engines like it when the link is embedded in words, not just a typed-out address.

Here is an example:

Bad- The site https://moz.com/beginners-guide-to-seo has some good tips for search engine optimization.

Good- The Moz site has some good tips for search engine optimization.

Just highlight the words and click on the link tool in the post editor or word processing software to embed your link.

# Consider Length

The length of your post or article makes a difference, too. Search engines seem to prefer posts that are 400 words or more. The longer, the better, though. Once again, search engines are looking for value.

If you have a post that is a gallery of images and very little words, don't worry. If there is a lot of media, it seems to cancel out the word count requirement.

## Long Content = Good Content, Most of the Time

There have been quite a few studies that discovered Google loves long form content. Long-form is any article or blog post that ranges from 700 words to 2000 words. Long articles are beloved by Google and the population at large because they give in-depth, nitty-gritty, wonderful details about a subject that people want. They aren't just a generic overview that most short article offer.

For example, I do a lot of writing for Live Science. A typical reference article for the site is broken down into sections that will cover every angle of the subject. Take this article on Earth Day that I wrote.

Before I wrote it, I brainstormed all of the things a person might ask about Earth Day, such as what is Earth Day, who started it, how successful it's been, who celebrates it now, etc. Then, I answered those questions in my article. It has been one of my most successful articles with more than 7,000 shares in just a little over 24 hours.

While I agree that long content does get a lot of search engine love and it gives readers what they want most of the time, you shouldn't get stuck on just adding long-form content to your site.

Why? Here are just a few reasons:

> People love variety. Your regular readers are going to get bored if you continually serve up articles that take 10 to 15 minutes to read.

> People love infographics! Sometimes people want an informative infographic they can skim, and search engines tend to rank infographics, too.

> There are times when people are just looking for a simple answer to their question. Don't go too short, though. Google sees pages with less than 200 words as "thin content."

# Be a Good Writer, Darn It!

Search engines also rank posts higher if they contain good spelling. This should go without saying, since you're a professional writer and all, but ALWAYS check your spelling.

That's It!

That's basically all writers need to know about SEO. Remember, as long as you're thinking about your reader and providing quality, then most of your worries are taken care of already.

# The Saga of Bogus SEO and Optimization Tactics

Now that you know what to do, I want to tell you what not to do. In fact, I want to shout it from the rooftops: Most of the SEO and optimization tactics you'll find online are utterly wrong!

I have talked with many website owners over the years, and it seems like they all have been drinking the same content Kool-Aid. You can't blame them for believing horrible optimization tactics. They were just hungry for some search engine love.

It's time to end the madness, though.

# Cutts Says Cut It Out with Article Directories

First, don't use article directories to build links. Oh, I've known so many people that have wandered into this trap...and then Google gave them the website smack down. Finally, Matt Cutts (official leader of everything Google SEO) of Google confirmed what I had always suspected a few years ago. Article directories are slimy, spammy places that gets your articles knocked down in the search engine abyss.

# Keywords Aren't as Important as Some People Think

Keywords were once the best way to draw search engine attention. That was a long time ago.

Search engines are smart enough that they can figure out what your content is about without a liberal smattering of keywords. Just add great content to your article and add keywords like I told you to earlier and things will be rosy. Trust me.

## Moral of the Story?

Make that blog or article or webpage shine! And if your client asks for bad SEO tactics, firmly tell them that you know what you're doing.

# Chapter 4: How to Create Quality Content

Now that you've got some of the basics down, let's dive into how to put an article or post together.

I've been around the block (over and over again) for two decades, so I know what content ranks and what content typically gets drowned out by everything else on the internet. I also know what readers love. Let me clear up some misconceptions and clue you into what's up with quality content.

## Build Your Quality with Layering

Rand over at Moz says that to rise to the top, you need content that's 10x better than everyone else's. I wouldn't go that far, but you do need to offer up content that no one else is serving.

Think about your favorite restaurant. You go there because it offers something its competitors don't, like better atmosphere, juicer burgers, tastier pasta or a finer selection of wine. It wouldn't be your favorite if it didn't stand out. Website content is the same. People, and search engines, love content that feeds their needs in a way that others can't.

To create content that stands out, you need a process that I call "content layering."

You start with a layer of beefy content. Pepper the text with helpful links, facts and data. Salt it with Click to Tweet quotes to make sharing easy.

Chop up some long text and turn it into a bulleted or numbered list for easy reading.

Slather on a layer of images rich with colors and interesting subject matter that's relevant to the text.

Finally, slap on a layer of audio or video content that will make visitors linger and savor your message.

The end result is a site post sandwich that satisfies and excites your visitors and search engine bots.

Mmm, mmm, good!

# Create Headlines that Catch Attention

Your article or blog post's headline is the first thing a reader sees. It needs to convey what the content is about and make the person want to read it.

Cute headlines are fun, but if they don't really give your reader a clear idea about what they're going to read, you've failed. They are going to click away.

Here are some tips for coming up with really solid headlines:

➢ Answer your readers question. A simple "How to Do XYZ" is often gold.

➢ Avoid using click-bait. Titles that scream controversy, offer incredible guarantees or apply similar cheap ploys, can serve a purpose, but only for a moment. If you do end up using click-bait headlines, you need to make sure the body of your copy backs it up in a big way.

➢ Grab the readers attention by revealing a shocking fact in your piece. "Your Sink is Filthier than Your Toilet" is a good example. Just make sure the title is true. No clickbait!

➢ Use numbers. For some reason, titles with numbers are big hits.

For example, my article "20 Unexpected Ways to Use Dryer Sheets" for CNET has garnered millions of views.

➢ Add urgency. Make your readers feel like this is information they need right now. For example: "Do These 10 Things Right Now to Increase Your Income" or "Don't Miss Out on These 5 Activities to Do This Weekend" or "This Writing Mistake is Costing You Clients."

➢ Tell your readers they are doing something wrong. For example, "You're Writing Your Headlines All Wrong" could be a good attention grabber. Make sure you follow up with how to fix the problem in the piece, or you just may make your readers mad.

➢ Add a little humor. "Annoying 2000s Tech We Kinda Miss" is a title example from one of my articles on No-FluffWriter.com.

- ➤ Keep your titles to 11 words or less. Long headlines are confusing.

- ➤ Put data in your headline. "50 Percent of Writers Don't Have XYZ" is an example of a data driven headline.

- ➤ Use words that show exactly what the format of the article encompasses, like how to, tips, lessons, guide, ideas, facts, strategies, secrets, gallery, collection, etc.

- ➤ Use unusual words. Fun use of words get attention and let the reader know this article isn't going to be boring. So, break out that thesaurus. Some of my favorites include awesomesauce, noob, heck, bountiful, heckling, gluttonous, baneful, wee, and assimilate.

- ➤ Use emotion. Add a little emotion to your headline with words like surprising, funny, shocking, maddening, stunning and helpful.

> Try to include who, what, when, where and how whenever you can.

Here are some examples from my articles:

By ALINA BRADFORD · CNET · December 22, 2015, 3:36 PM

**True or false? Ridiculous microwave myths you can stop believing**

taking action

# 21 Tools For Classy Ladies Who Like To Code

We ain't afraid of no Python.

by **mtv news staff** 8m ago

*By Alina Bradford*

Even though women make up around half of the workforce, they only occupy a little less than 25 percent of science, technology, engineering and math (STEM) jobs. This statistic doesn't mean that the guys are better at STEM jobs, it just means that more

CBS News | CBS Evening News | CBS This Morning | 48 Hours | 60 Minutes | Sunday Morning | Face The Nation

⊙CBSNEWS    Video  US  World  Politics  Entertainment  Health  MoneyWatch

By ALINA BRADFORD · CNET · July 7, 2016, 11:31 AM

# How to tell if your Facebook has been hacked, and what you can do about it

## Angies list

Quick Tour | FAQ | In the Press | Articles | The Big Deal | Business Owners

### Be cautious of online travel planners

#### Using a travel agent

Several travel agents on Angie's List share the benefits of using this service as well as the pitfalls of planning a trip without a professional agent.

A travel agent prevents disaster vacations

Ili states a travel agent can prevent

**Be cautious of online travel planners**

Travel agents consider the kids

**Date Published:** Oct 02 2012
*by Alina Bradford, Angie's List Contributor*

The advertisements for websites online and on television claim to make trip planning easy and affordable, but they're not necessarily better than working through a travel agent. Russell J Vara, a Charlotte travel agent at Maestro Travel, offers the opposing view.

By using an online company to plan your trip, you aren't saving as much as you think you are. Russell contends. Online mega sites like Priceline, Orbitz and Expedia have gigantic advertising budgets and they use these budgets to convince the consumer that they're getting a substantially better deal by booking all their arrangements themselves -- but their prices are the same as what any travel agency can get you.

## 5 things to do with your old phone (other than sell it)

If you stop having the latest phone, then you probably have a couple of perfectly good phones sitting in a desk drawer or in a closet. They aren't really worth enough to sell, but they still work, so throwing them away isn't an option, either.

It's time to give those old-offs a new purpose. Here are five ideas to take your old phone from junk drawer fodder to productive member of your household.

**Turn it into a security camera**

If the camera is still good on your old phone, turning it into a security camera is an option. With it, you can keep an eye on your back door, use it as a baby monitor or spy on your pets.

Taylor Martin has a great tutorial on how to turn old phones into a home security camera you can watch from anywhere.

**Donate it to science (sort of)**

Even if you don't want to use your old phone, someone else might. There are a couple apps

## 11 REASONS POLAROID IS MAKING A COMEBACK

### TIME TO MAKE IT SNAPPY.

MTV NEWS STAFF ✎
09/13/2016

By Alina Bradford

When we heard that Polaroid is coming out with a digital camera that prints photos, we have to admit, we got a little giddy. Any kid born in the '80s or '90s kinda

---

   cnet   BEST PRODUCTS  REVIEWS  NEWS  VIDEO  HOW TO  SMART HOME  CARS  DEALS  DOWNLOAD                            Q

SMART HOME

## What do those clothing label symbols actually mean?

Hint: Pay attention to those symbols on the clothing label.

BY ALINA BRADFORD | MARCH 4, 2016 3:04 PM PST

f  ✎  P  ⊕  ⏍

---

⅛ Scripted                                                          Who W

Blog Home / Content Marketing / Alina Bradford / 3 Publishers Rocking Sponsored Content

## 3 Publishers Rocking Sponsored Content

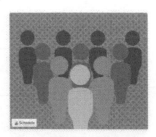

**NewCo Shift**

LATEST STORIES

Facebook Plans to Privacy-Why?
March 13, 2019

The Internet Must Change, So Get
There, Start With the Data.
January 29, 2019

Predictions for 2019: Data, Tech,
Media, Climate, Markets and
Cannabis.
January 2, 2019

One Year Ago: How Our Predictions
Fared

# Avert Disaster by Backing Up Your Salesforce Data

By Anna-Bradford

### Get Shift Done: Tips and Tricks

Sites go down. Employees make mistakes. Your cat sits on the computer. That's why you need to make sure your important Salesforce data is backed up—just in case.

# Add a Dek

A dek is a little line below the headline that gives readers a little more information about what they're about to read. Most websites use deks, written out in sentence form.

To write a successful dek, remember to add to the title, add information, be creative, but be a little bit of a tease, too. Boring deks can drive your readers away.

Here's some examples of decent deks:

Title: You're Thinking too Much About Keywords

Dek: If you're doing this with your keywords you may be making the Google gods angry.

Title: How to Use Deks in an Article

Dek: They're more important than you may think.

Title: You Aren't Doing Your Article Updates Correctly

Dek: Miss these few steps and you'll probably lose your reader.

# Avoid Fluffy Content: It's Bad Customer Service

I'm called the No-Fluff Writer for a reason. I preach getting to the heart of the topic right away. Make sure you follow the No-Fluff ways. Don't put fluff in your articles!

What is fluff? Fluff is content that really isn't saying anything helpful. It's basically used to puff up the word count to appease the SEO Google gods, or a demanding client. Are you giving your clients and readers bad customer service by creating content that doesn't have enough meat?

Think about it while I tell you a little story.

# Fluff and Angry Customers

Facebook one day and I saw a post by a popular women's magazine. I liked the title and preview linked in the post, so I clicked and read the article. IT. WAS. BAD.

The article was supposed to be about laundry secrets you just must learn ASAP. The article, though, gave washed up (no pun intended), old advice that anyone within their target audience would already know. A few old tips and done. Nothing meaty and useful to the reader.

I was curious to see what others thought of the article, so I clicked back to Facebook and looked at the comments on the post. Almost every single comment was about how basic the article was and how the title was very misleading.

Over the next week or so, I started checking the comments on other articles. The articles that I felt didn't live up to their title or gave simple information that most people already know had so many negative comments. What really shocked me was the multiple offenders. These publications continually drew in readers with flashy titles, then served up mediocre articles that left their readers yawning, confused, or even worse, angry.

Don't make your customers mad with crappy content.

Angry readers matter, my friends. Many of those ticked-off readers that I came across voted with their clicks. In the comments, they stated that they were unfollowing the website and/or canceling their subscriptions.

You know it didn't stop there, right? Those angry people probably told their friends, which probably lead to more bad feelings towards the website and the brand.

## How to Stop the Fluff

Articles or blog posts aren't just a great way to bring in views to your site or your client's site.

They are, in a way, a customer service. Sure, you aren't talking directly to potential customers to complete or help with a transaction, but you are talking to your customers. You're providing a service with your content.

If you don't spend time crafting a great piece that will be interesting to your readers and delivers on the promise made in the title, then you're giving them poor customer service.

I don't need to tell you that poor customer service makes you lose customers. You know that already.

# Give Customers What They Want: Great Content!

Remember that content sandwich from earlier? Here's the elements of a meaty article:

➢ Research in the form of quotes or data

➢ Tips that are different from the million other articles on the web on the same topic

➢ A personal story to illustrate a point

➢ Testimonials

➢ Media like gifs, photos, graphs and videos

There is no reason for posting fluff. Just don't do it. Give your customers what they want.

# Watch Out for Fluffy Headlines, Too

Many websites draw in visitors from social media sites with sensational headlines, but then fail to deliver in the content.

This is called click-baiting and it results in loss of trust from your visitors. They bounce before clicking on anything else on your site. This, in turn, impacts your conversion rates.

You don't need to have a sensationalist headline to let your readers down, though. Any content that doesn't answer the specific question that the headline promises is poor content.

# Fight Generic Content: How to Create Interesting Posts

I was recently critiquing a person's article, and something struck me. This article had everything going for it...in theory. It was on a great topic that would be interesting to the reader. The problem was, once you started reading, it was clear that the article was generic.

It was a general dabbling into the subject and not the in-depth article the title promised. Of course, the average reader would click away from the article right away and never come back to the site.

To help you avoid this mistake, I'm going to give you a sure-fire way to determine if your content is generic with one easy step.

## How to Spot a Generic Article

Spotting a generic article is easy. All you need to do is see if you can swap your main keyword for something else.

For example, say your article was entitled: How Marketers Can Use PayPal.

Throughout your article, you should give examples of how marketers, specifically, can use PayPal. If you can switch out the word "marketers" and replace it with any other type of profession, then your article is generic.

# How to Fix
# Generic Content

Fixing generic content is just as easy as spotting it. Simply go through your article and insert tips or ideas that are specific to your topic keyword. Remember, you want people to learn or be entertained with tidbits that pertain to their interests. If they aren't learning or being entertained, then your article is nothing but search fodder.

Nothing makes me angrier than search fodder. That's articles that are created with the sole intent of drawing in hits through keyword usage. These articles are dry, useless and infuriating because they waste people's time. Not to mention, search engines are looking for helpful content more than keywords and SEO tricks these days, anyway.

Keep it classy. Make sure that your content avoids the generic label and is something special. Not only will your brand gain a loyal following, you'll also get more search engine love.

# Chapter 5: Proofreading Techniques

We've been over grammar and spelling in a previous chapter, but I want to talk about the best methods of catching those mistakes in this chapter. Here are a few ways to spot typos before they make it you're your editor, audience or client.

## Use Google Translate to Proofread Your Writing (Seriously!)

They say one of the best ways to find errors in your blog posts, book or articles is to read the sentences out loud. An even better method is to have someone else read your piece out loud. This can be difficult if you're a typical writer, alone in your home office.

No problem. A bot can help.

You can use Google Translate as you're editing co-worker. Best of all, it's free.

Just go to the tool at https://translate.google.com. Then, copy and paste your text into the box on the left. Finally, click the sound button to hear your work read aloud.

# Read Back-to-Front

Another way to catch typos is to read your paragraphs backwards. I know this doesn't make any sense. How can you catch errors if you're not reading the sentences the way they are intended, right? Trust me. It works.

# Read No Less than Three Times

I've made a rule to always check over my work three times before submitting. The times I haven't followed my rule? Yep, there were problems.

# Take a Timeout

Before you look over your work one last time, take a breather. Let it marinate as long as you can, then come back. You'll look at the piece with fresh eyes and will notice things you missed before.

# You'll Make Mistakes

Oh, writer my friend, you will make mistakes. Even with all of the editing and trying and revising you do, you'll put "your" when you mean "you're" or "were" when you mean "where."

When you do, the world will be sure to point it out and try to make you feel like less of a writer. Don't let it bring you down. Everyone, even seasoned professionals, make mistakes.

I mean, look at Christopher Columbus. He went to a whole different continent than intended and named the indigenous people Indians, even though they looked nothing like Indians. Huge screw-up on a historical level!

I myself make typos a lot more often than I'd like to admit. Even though this book has been edited probably several dozen times by the time you read it, you'll undoubtedly still find something that isn't perfect.

That's true of most books. Even ones produced my major publishers. (Don't believe me? Go read a book on The New York Times Best Seller list.)

A while back I corrected a typo in an Instagram post and still used the wrong spelling. People were quick to let me know about it.

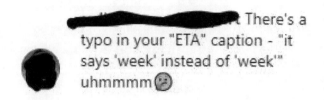

There's a typo in your "ETA" caption - "it says 'week' instead of 'week'" uhmmmm😣

Mistakes don't make you a bad writer. As long as you make sure that you make as few errors as possible and work hard to make your writing interesting and informative, you'll end up being very successful.

Don't let the fear of errors keep you from writing!

# Chapter 6: Speedy Writing Tips for Beginners

Like I've said, I've been in the game of content marketing for, well, a bunch of years. One thing that I've learned well is how to write a blog post and write it quickly. Hey, when you're getting paid by the post, you learn how to be fast!

So, I thought I'd share with my readers my tips for going from an idea to a published post in less than 60 minutes. Got those timers ready? Get ready. Get set. Go!

## Reference at Your Fingertips

There are many sites made specifically to aid writers on their quest for information, resources, and education. Below are some of the best to help you save time and get writing.

Everyone knows that you need a good dictionary, thesaurus and encyclopedia, but thumbing through these can waste huge masses of time. Besides, why buy these reference books when you can easily access them on the web? This saves time and money!

Here are a few you should bookmark in your browser:

➢ Merriam and Webster Online is the best online resources for spelling help and a thesaurus.

➢ Encyclopedia Britannica has in-depth knowledge almost every topic you can think of when doing research. It also has links to other helpful resources.

➢ Writer's Market.com is the digital version of this long-time writer's staple offers instant access to thousands of editors and agents just for a few dollars a month. This is a great time saver because it is constantly being updated. No more getting returned query letters because of address changes or business mergers.

# Speedy Research

Doing research is one of the biggest time eaters there is for writers. Going to the library can take up a whole day. And typing random terms into search engines can be just as time consuming.

Finding several surefire research sites is the best way to maximize writing time. The key is to stay focused on your topic.

Say you are looking for information on the best places to go salmon fishing. You find several great articles on salmon fishing, but a few popups about salmon recipes. Even if you are tempted, don't stray over to other topics that may pique you interest. Stay focused! It saves precious time that you need to write your story.

Need really detailed information like statistics or government documents for your story? Don't schlep to your local government agency.

Here's some sites:

➢ Use Fedstats and USA.gov for demographic information.

➢ Go to the Centers for Disease Control and Prevention (CDC) website for information and statistics about diseases

➢ Use Profnet to find experts for quotes.

➢ Head over to the Mayo Clinic Online for facts about almost any illness you can think of.

➢ Search the World Health Organization website for world-wide information about illnesses, pandemics, epidemics and more.

➢ Go to the US Food and Drug Administration (FDA) website for facts about drug testing, current treatments on the market, food safety and more.

➢ Use the World Bank Open Data site for statistics on countries.

There are more sites listed in the Appendix.

# Easy Steps to Writing a Blog Post in Just Minutes

## Figure Out Your Topic

Don't know what to write? Take a look at what others in your field are writing about to brainstorm some ideas using BuzzSumo. Here is a more traditional way to brainstorm, too.

Time: 5 to 10 minutes

## Do Your Research

You've got a fantastic idea, but don't start typing yet. First, plug the topic into Google's Keyword Planner to decide which keywords will be best for your post. Don't get too caught up in picking, just choose a couple that have low or medium competition but have high monthly search (over 20,000 searches are ideal).

Time: 5 minutes

## Summarize Your Content

To make the writing process as fast as possible, summarize the different parts of your post you want to talk about and then use them as your H2 headers.

Time: 5 minutes

Sometimes I look like this when I'm writing a blog post.

## Fill in the Blanks

Now that you have your headers, fill in the blanks until you talk about everything you wanted to cover in the post.

Time: 15 to 20 minutes

## Finish Up

Now, write the intro, the closing paragraph and the call to action. Once you have those wrapped up, don't forget to write a meta description.

Time: 10 to 15 minutes

## Add Some Media

Add some flash (and some search engine love) to your post by adding some media. Search for free content or create your own using. Remember these from earlier?

- Giphy for GIFs
- Creative Commons for Creative Common photos
- YouTube for embeddable videos
- Easel.ly for infographics
- Meme Generator
- Pablo for quotes
- PhotoPin for Creative Commons photos
- DaFont for fonts
- Office Sway for presentations
- Pond5 for historic media files
- Survey Monkey for surveys
- NVD3 for charts
- Mapbox for maps
- OpenClipArt for clip art
- GetEmojis for emojis
- Pexels for modern, clean photos

➢ PhotoPin finds Creative Commons photos

➢ Pexel Videos for free stock videos

➢ ClipSafari for clipart

➢ MyEcoverMaker to create covers for ebooks

➢ Unsplash for free stock photos

Time: 10 minutes

That's all there's to my process. Pretty simple, huh? Trust me, once you get the hang of it, you can crank out blog posts in just 15 to 30 minutes without breaking a sweat!

# When Things Get Hard, Use an Article Quality Checklist

Stupid mistakes are my nemesis when my mind is distracted. The best thing to do is to try your best, but also fall back on a checklist to be sure you didn't miss anything before you submit the work. It's the fast way to catch mistakes.

This checklist will help you create quality articles and blog posts, no matter what type of stress you're facing.

- ✦ Does the title make sense?

- ✦ Is the title in the right style of capitalization for the publication? For example, are all the words capitalized? Or just this first?

- ✦ Does the title have good flow and include keywords?

- ✧ Take out the unnecessary "that" words found in your article.

- ✧ Check your "it's" and "its" to make sure they are correct.

- ✧ Are the headers in H3 or H2, depending on your client's requirements?

- ✧ Are there enough photos?

- ✧ Did you meet the word count requirement, if there is one?

- ✧ Take a look at all of the "an" and "a" words in your article. If they come before a word with a vowel, remember the it should be "an" not "a."

- ✧ Did you link to any sources or cite your sources correctly, depending on the needs of the client?

- ✧ Do all your sentences flow well? Remember to mix compound sentences and simple sentences throughout a paragraph to make the rhythm interesting.

✧ Make sure your paragraphs transition well.

✧ Are all of the sentences punctuated correctly?

✧ Cut any repetitions or unneeded words. (Remember, no fluff!)

✧ Does the overall theme fit the idea of the article, or did you go off track?

✧ Did you break down complicated steps into numbered lists?

✧ Did you make a group of items into bulleted lists for easy reading?

✧ If your article or blog has keywords, did you make sure to use them naturally, so they don't seem awkward?

✧ Is there a Call to Action or something to lead the reader to another page?

✧ Did you use first, second or third person throughout?

- ✧ Is the article or blog the right tone? Is it too formal or too casual, for example?

- ✧ Pretend you've never read this post before and know little about the subject. Is any of it confusing?

- ✧ Are there any videos or gifs you can embed to make the post more interesting?

- ✧ Did you include easy ways to follow you on social media though call-to-action or follow buttons?

# Chapter 7: Brainstorming Ideas

The worst part of running a writing business is when you don't have any ideas for an article or post. It's that oh s**t moment.

No matter what sort of writer you are, you'll get blocked sometimes. Even JK Rowling suffered terrible writer's block when she was trying to write Harry Potter and the Chamber of Secrets. Luckily there are a few things you can do to get yourself through writer's block and back into a creative frame of mind.

## Get Away from the Desk

If your writer's block is just a momentary thing and you haven't been suffering for months, the best thing to do is to get up from your desk and go for a walk.

Whether you get a cup of tea and go to sit outside for half an hour, or you strap on your walking boots and get down and dirty with nature for an afternoon, is up to you - but it's important to change your environment.

You could even move your laptop to a different place in the house for a slightly different perspective. I like to sit at my patio table in my yard.

# Try Free Writing

Pick up a pen and paper and write for fifteen minutes without stopping, even if your hand starts to cramp up. If you have an obliging friend, ask them to read out words to you for inspiration.

Although a lot of what you write won't be useful in the slightest, chances are there will be a few phrases in there that will be interesting simply because you didn't have a chance to think about them before you wrote them down. Free writing can show you what's really in your head by lowering your inhibitions.

# Experience Other Stories

If you're suffering from an ability to structure your writing, why not take in other people's stories? Watch a great season of TV or a movie in a similar genre. For example, if you're writing a gangster novel, watch the likes of The Godfather and The Sopranos.

# Do a Throwback

For bloggers, sometimes, to create great content you don't need to create new content. One look at your former posts can supply you with a plethora of awesome future posts.

For example, do a roundup of your most popular posts. Go to your site stats and take a look at the posts that got the most views, the most comments or the most shares. Choose the top ten and create a post that links to each other with a brief description of why each post rocks. Better yet, add your favorite line or tip from each post to the description.

Another idea for repurposing old posts is by expanding on them. Do an update or flesh out the old post with new or more complex information.

For example, on one of my sites (I sold the site in 2014) I wrote a post on how to draw people. Then I broke that general information post down into more in-depth posts, such as How to Draw a Child, How to Draw a Nose, How to Draw a Mouth, and a dozen other posts.

# Mind Maps

Another way to find ideas, do a brainstorming session with mind maps. Draw a circle on a piece of paper and write the name of the post in the circle.

Now draw some smaller circles around the large one. Fill these circles with topics that stem from the main topic in the main post.

Branch out from these ideas with circles with even more detailed ideas.

Here is an example:

# Do a Survey

If you want 100% new ideas for your blog or articles, then mine your readers. Set up a survey (SurveyMonkey is a good app to use) and ask them about what their biggest concerns are. Then, craft posts that answer their questions or concerns. This one tactic can give you a lot of great topics to work with and the best part is your readers will really care about your posts.

# Read Books

Another super helpful tactic is reading the posts of other people in your industry. You may find that you have such a strong reaction to something you read that you simply must write a rebuttal.

Here is an example:

Neal Frankle says that going to college can be a waste of time and money. While in some cases I would agree, my own experience has shown me that even half a degree can be worth your while.

One post can even spawn ideas for several others. I took the one post by Neal Frankle and used it to spur ideas for another post for one of my clients.

# Read Poetry

One of the great things about poetry is that each one is like a short story - a poem is a representation of a thought on the page instead of a long, labored plot structure. If you're having problems writing and you're feeling jealous of other writers, you could read some poetry from the older Romantic poets like Wordsworth to more recent poets like the spoken word poet Andrea Gibson.

Reading poetry will help you appreciate the beauty and

importance of carefully choosing each word and it will help you write sentence by sentence instead of thinking of your article as an enormous task that you will inevitably fail at.

# Listen to Music

Crank up your favorite jam and rock out. The burst of feel good chemicals can get your brain working.

If that doesn't work, try listing to a genre that you usually don't like or listen to. The change may be enough to startle your brain into work mode.

# Brainstorm by Sleeping

Some of the greatest ideas have come about by sleeping. American author John Steinbeck wrote, "A problem difficult at night is resolved in the morning after the committee of sleep has worked on it."

Many other great minds have felt the same way about the power of sleep. Einstein's theory of relativity supposedly began with a dream about a field full of cows surrounded by an electric fence. The song "Yesterday", drifted to Paul McCartney while he slept in 1964 and The Terminator came to director James Cameron in a dream many years later.

The periodic table came to the Russian chemist Dmitri Mendeleev in his sleep in 1869. "I saw in a dream a table where all the elements fell into place as required," he wrote. "Awakening, I immediately wrote it down on a piece of paper. Only in one place did a correction later seem necessary."

How can you harness the power of sleep?

➤ Ask yourself a question before you go to sleep or focus on the problem at hand.

➤ Set timers so that you'll wake up throughout the night. Both Salvador Dalí and Thomas Edison would be sure to get woken up just as they drifted off to capture ideas.

➢ Keep a notebook beside your bed so you can write any revelations down when you wake up.

➢ Practice lucid dreaming. This is a difficult skill of being aware while you're dreaming. There are several good books on the topic.

# Focus on a Writing Project Outside Your Comfort Zone

We also tend to get caught doing the same jobs. It makes sense for security purposes, but it can also lead to blockages. If you're writing the same articles from different angles, it's no wonder your ideas have stopped flowing.

If you're struggling, accept it and step away. It may mean losing some money, but it allows you to focus on something else. And, that could be a Godsend.

This could involve anything. You may want to write a story instead of a news piece, or a poem instead of fiction. You may even want to spread your love of words in schools. In this instance, you could start a school magazine and distribute it.

# Learn a New Craft

If crafts get your juices flowing, it may be time to put down the pen altogether.

Learning a new craft, like knitting, allows you to keep creativity flowing, while also learning something new. Since knitting is a relatively passive craft, it leaves your mind free to come up with new ideas.

## Get a New Active Hobby

Being active pumps happy chemicals to your brain. These chemicals can make you more creative, leading to great ideas you never thought of before.

# Chapter 8: Take My 30-Day Blog Challenge

Now that you know the basics of web writing, let's practice with this 30-day challenge. It will build your skillset and help you create content that you can show to potential clients.

Let's get started!

# DAY 1

Today is all about building the foundation. Start by brain dumping every post idea you can think of into a notebook. There are no stupid ideas, but make sure you stay on topic.

If your site is about bathroom products don't write down post ideas that revolve around gardening, for example. Need help with ideas? Take a look at this brainstorming help.

# DAY 2

Now that you have a list of possible post topics, go through and pick out your top eight ideas. That will give you two posts per week for a month.

# DAY 3

In your notebook, make a page for each article idea. Write an idea at the top of each page. On the pages write out a few lines about what each post would cover. This is another time to brain dump!

# DAY 4

Now is the time to write your first post. Write an introduction, and then write a subheading for every item you want to talk about in the post. This will get your thoughts organized.

Fill in the information in detail and then sum everything up at the end. After your closing paragraph add a CTA (Call to Action.) You can see an example of a CTA at the end of this post.

# DAY 5

Now that you have a post, go over it and check for spelling and grammar mistakes. Then, give it a rocking title.

# DAY 6

Pick some photos for your post. Make sure you save the photos with keyword-rich terms and give them a title, caption, alt text and description that is also keyword-rich. This will help with your ranking.

Also, the more photos you have, the better, so pick at least two images to accompany your post.

# DAY 7

Post that post! You're ready to fly! Use a site like Buffer to set up a schedule for social media links to your new content. You'll want a link to post right away, one in eight hours, one in 24 hours, on in a week and one in a month on Twitter. On other social media sites, post once immediately and then once again in a month or so.

# DAY 8

Okay, you've got a great post under your belt. Now what? Start on the next post! Now that you know how, you can start writing your posts at a faster rate. Write the whole post out today!

# DAY 9

Great content isn't just about text posts. Visuals are amazing tools for getting pageviews and loyal fans.

So, today, take a video of yourself talking about your brand or a great product you offer. Post it to YouTube and embed it to create a new post on your site.

# DAY 10

A sample of infographics that can be made over at easel.ly.

Another great visual to add to your site is infographics. You can create your own infographics for free at easel.ly. Use one of the blog topic ideas that you didn't use for inspiration for your infographic.

# DAY 11

Remember that post you wrote on Day 8? Post that sucker!

# DAY 12

Get to work on your next blog post.

# DAY 13

A good way to boost your site rank is to check the amount of text on all your posts and pages. Google considers a page or post with less than 200 words not worth people's time. Write down a list of all the pages that need a boost in content.

# DAY 14

Choose two pages from the list you made yesterday and add some content to them.

# DAY 15

Post your blog post that you wrote on Day 11.

# DAY 16

Write your next blog post.

# DAY 17

Dead or broken links can lower your page rank. Use a tool like Broken Link Checker by Janis Elsts to find and fix broken links.

# DAY 18

Make another video post. Concentrate on showing your personality while you talk.

# DAY 19

Get Day 16's post up on your blog.

# DAY 20

Write your next post.

# DAY 21

Choose two pages from the list you made on Day 13 and add some content to those pages.

# DAY 22

Make it easier for visitors to share your content. Add social media sharing buttons to your site. I personally like Flare. Only link to three different social media sites, though. This gives you better interaction by not overwhelming your readers with choices.

# DAY 23

Have a social media Q and A. Invite people on social media to ask you questions for an hour and answer the questions in real time. Be sure to link to any posts you have that will give a more in-depth answer.

# DAY 24

Post Day 20th's blog post.

# DAY 25

Write your next post.

# DAY 26

Video post day! Make a post about why you started your business and how you hope it will help your customers.

# DAY 27

Choose two pages from the list you made on Day 13 and add some content to those pages.

# DAY 28

Get your meta descriptions for your pages and posts in sparkling condition. Make it easy by using a plugin like Yoast.

# DAY 29

Post Day 25th's blog post.

You made it across the finish line! Good job!

# DAY 30

Write your next blog post.

You did it!

Congratulations on finishing a whole month of content creation and clean up! You should be seeing more pageviews, better ranking on search engines and more interaction in the comments section and on social media.

# Chapter 9: What Not to Do to Make Money

Okay, we're done with learning the finer points of writing. From now on in the book, we're going to focus on getting clients and making money.

Before I tell you what to do, I think it is important to tell you what not to do. If you know what to avoid, then you won't make nearly as many mistakes as I did.

Let's get started.

## For the Love of God, Don't Write for Free

As a freelancer, you'll see job ads that say things like, "We don't pay, but this job is great exposure" or "Your work will be seen by our many followers, which will be great way to get your work seen." This is hogwash, sir. Utter hogwash. Never in the history of freelance writing has anyone ever gotten a gig from a dinky site promising exposure.

Sure, if you can get a byline from a huge site that doesn't pay freelance writers, like Huffington Post, you may snag a paying gig. Don't count on it, though.

To this day, I still get offers to write for sites and publications for exposure. This is an email I got just the other day, in fact:

*Dear Alina,*

*Our team at Destination Luxury came across your profile on LinkedIn and your writing experience caught our attention. We believe your given experience is what we are seeking in our writers and would like to know if you would be interested in joining our team as a contributor for Destination Luxury.*

*Destination Luxury is a publication focused on the luxury market. Our mission is to capture the most exclusive locales, events and people in alluring, poignant and inspiring features. Reaching millions of people through our digital platforms, we are an established leader in the luxury sector.*

*By contributing to Destination Luxury, you have the opportunity to build your portfolio of professional work. Destination Luxury has nearly 300,000 followers on Facebook and over 31,000 followers on Instagram and Twitter, and as a contributing writer, you may gain exposure to these followers.*

*If you are interested in the position, please feel free to email us for further information regarding the company and to , schedule a phone call to discuss this opportunity.*

*Best Wishes,*

*Lady who made me laugh*

This was my reply:

*I would love to talk. What is your budget per article? I my current clients pay $200 to $1,000 per article.*

*Thanks again for your interest.*

*I never got a response. Big surprise!*

*Sometimes they try to get creative. I've seen publications try to pay writers with cookies, candy or free lessons of some sort. Anything to save a buck.*

Here's one of my favorites:

---

**✷ content writer needed**

I am seeking a writer of content for a new vaporizer I am putting on the market as well as future products I am putting together. I would like to barter marijuana for this at this time but there is a potential for $ in the near future.

• do NOT contact me with unsolicited services or offers

---

Yep. That guy is trying to get people to write in exchange for pot.

By saying no to these people, don't even for one second think that you are missing out on a possible opportunity. You're not. You're just going to waste your time working for free when you could have been doing something productive for your career.

You won't be alone in rejecting these offers. Freelancers who make the big bucks know that writing for free is a no-go.

Here are some royalty-free replies you can send people who offer you experience:

I tried to feed my kid experience, but he's allergic to it.

I told my landlord I'd pay him with all the experience I'll be getting and he laughed at me. So, I'll need money, please.

You can't tuck experience into a stripper's g-string, dude.

My 20s were rough. I have enough experience to last me a lifetime.

# Skip the Content Mills, too

90% of job ads are for content mills that pay something like $3 for 500 words. Hey, at least you're getting paid, right?

Uh, no.

You would need to write a little more than 3 articles per hour to make $10 an hour, which probably isn't even a living wage where you live. And even if it is, your brain will get so fried by the time you made enough to buy a bag of groceries that you'll never want to look at a keyboard again.

Just.

Say.

No.

# Chapter 10: Make and Sharpen Your Tools

Before you start selling yourself as a freelancer, you need tools. Once you have those tools, you need to wow.

## Decide on Your Niche...or Two or Three

Before you can do anything as a freelance writer, you need to decide on your niche. No matter if you want to write copy for emails and sales pages or you want to write articles for websites, you need a specialty. This will set you apart from Joe Whoever that writes whatever pays. Clients are looking for people that genuinely love the same things they do.

You don't have to choose just one and you don't need to always write in your niche. Hell, I don't. Still, you need three or less topics to focus on. It will keep you focused and potential clients interested.

# Assignment: Choose Your Niche

Here's your first assignment: Choose 1 to 3 topics as your niche.

-First, write a list of all the topics you love. The category could be as simple as toy trains or as broad as lifestyle or fashion.

For inspiration, think about:

➤ Your hobbies

➤ The type of magazines you subscribe to

➢ Things you love to talk about with your friends or co-workers

➢ The articles you like to read on the internet

➢ The blogs you follow

-From that list, circle all the topics that you feel you are at least somewhat knowledgeable about.

-Finally, close your eyes and imagine writing every day for the next year on your circled topics. Could you do it? Cross out any of the circled topics that would bore you to tears after a few months.

Now, you should have a very short list of topics that excite you and you could write about competently, with a little research.

# Hone Your Brand

Your brand is what makes you stand out from the crowd. Before you can go any further, you need to understand what makes you special. For your first lesson, I'd like to talk about the meaning of life. No, I don't know the meaning of life. I wish I did! I do know what life isn't, though. Life isn't a contest.

Often, when freelancers start to visualize their brand they think about all of the other competitors out on the market. They wonder how they can be the best.

They are going about their branding process all wrong.

Each night I try to write an inspirational quote or a tidbit of knowledge that I've gleaned along the way on the bathroom mirror for my girls to see before they head off to school the next morning. One night, I wrote:

There is always going to be someone smarter, prettier, faster, etc. Be the best YOU can be. Life isn't a contest.

I think too many people get caught up in what everybody else is doing and they don't focus enough on what makes their brand special. Notice I said "special" and not "better."

Proving you're better than someone else is like trying to prove you love your spouse to someone who doesn't know you. You can show them all the proof in the world, but they still won't be 100% sure. That's because all humans are just a little suspicious of each other. In the back of our minds we're wondering if that guy really loves his wife or if he's cheating with Ms. Robertson next door. It's the same with businesses. They say they're the best, but are they just full of hot air?

When people look at your branding, don't make them wonder if you're just full of hot air. Give them a positive feeling and you are off to a great start. Get them to laugh or feel nostalgic or feel at home. That's what branding is all about. Conveying a feeling right off the bat and threading that feeling through everything that you present to your customer.

# Assignment: What's Your Brand?

I'm going to ask you some questions. Answer them as honestly as possible. Let's get started.

Will you be the face of your freelance business? For example, I am the face of my company. In fact, my company name is my own personal name. My company is 100% my voice and no one else's. Another example would be Dave Thomas of Wendy's. The restaurant was named after his daughter and her face was the logo, but he was the one that stared in many of the early commercials. His face, voice and sense of humor were what cemented Wendy's brand.

If you don't want your freelance business to center around you, no problem. We can work with that! You just need to know how you are going to present your business to the world.

Will you have a logo instead of a professional photo to represent your business?

Will your business be your name or will you come up with something else to call it?

What colors will represent your business? Remember, branding needs consistency.

What do you think is special about you? For example, do you have a passion for the environment and want to be seen as a "green" freelancer? Could your former job give you an interesting insight into your niche that you could capitalize on?

# Get the Sizzle: 5 Steps for Building Your Brand Identity with Your Website

Building your brand identity starts with your website. Everything you add to your site will affect how visitors will feel about your freelance writing business. Revamping your site to create a more cohesive brand is the best way to boost sales and make customers remember you.

## Branding with Colors

Step one is the most visual way to brand your site. Using one or two colors throughout your site, marketing items and packaging creates is more than just making things matchy-matchy. It gives consumers a visual clue as to who you are.

It has even been proven that colors can influence purchases. So, choose one or two colors that will represent your business, ideally colors already used in your logo.

## Branding with Font

Like colors, you need to pick two to three fonts, tops, that will be used on your site. Mimic the font used on your packaging or in your logo for headers or H1 titles. Be sure that your page text is easily readable, though.

## Branding with Your Logo

Now, your logo isn't just for the header of your website. Use it throughout. Watermark images with it. Use it on your about page. Use it in the footer. Be sure that you use it throughout your site.

# Branding with Images

Have you ever been to a website that uses images that all seem to go together? That theme is their image brand. If you visit my site often, you'll probably notice that I use a lot of GIFs and fun images. I like to keep things light while talking about serious subjects. That's my brand.

You can do it, too. Come up with a theme for your images and be consistent. For example, product images could all have the same background or images could all work together in a common theme such as nature, modernism, zen, etc.

# Branding with Content Tone

Once you have the visuals in place, concentrate on the tone of your text. Every article, blog post, content description, etc, should have the same tone. Don't bounce from fun and peppy to straight-laced and staunch. Stay the same. Let consumers know who you are. Build a personality through your text.

# 6 Ways to Make Your Site Traffic Soar

Now that you have branding down, it's time to get traffic to your website so you can pick up customer. These tips will also help you learn how to draw in traffic for your customers.

## Update Your Content

With changes in rules, regulations, laws and the way technology are advancing at an amazing pace, something you wrote on your website 6 months ago could be totally out of date and mislead anyone that reads it. You need to reread all of the past articles and blogs and update any of them that fall into this category. Search engines will see the post as still being relevant and that can help with your SEO rankings.

- A good update includes:
- A new title
- New intro paragraph
- Two links to other content on your site in the intro paragraph
- Broken links are fixed
- More media, if you can find some good stuff
- Publish it as a new article, but leave the address the same

## Use Ads to Move Up the Rankings

Most times, when you put something into your search engine, the top few results will say 'ad' at the side. This is because businesses have paid to be in one of the top spots.

Getting your own ad can be well worth the money invested because then your page is much more likely to be linked to by viewers, raising your rank.

## Make the Most of Social Media

Social media is a must for all businesses. It's a vital way of getting your brand known and an awesome way to send more traffic to your website.

You should post every day, at least, but do not make all your posts promotional. If you do, users will start to scroll past your posts without bothering to read them.

One promotional post out of five is a good rule of thumb. Some people post 20 percent promotional content and 80 percent other content. Your mix will depend on your target audience.

Don't just use memes, photos and text posts, either. Videos are sometimes the best way to attract attention to your brand, and if they contain some humor, they are likely to be shared.

Also, always respond to any comments in a positive manner. This will help to build trust in your business and make you look like a professional. Nobody wants to deal with rudeness.

Be sure to put a link to your site on all your posts to drive traffic. On Instagram, using your website address as a watermark is a good idea.

## Email Marketing

Email marketing fell out of favor for a while but now it is back. It is a great way to stay connected with existing customers or to make connections with new ones.

To be effective, each email has to be interesting or solve a problem for your audience, and it should always have a link to your website included.

## Run a Contest

Running a contest is a great way to attract new traffic. You just have to make sharing a link to your site one of the rules of entry. Another smart rule is they must enter with their email address so you can add this to your mailing list.

## Optimize for Mobile

Around 80 percent of internet use is done on mobile devices. This percentage is likely to grow, I mean, smart phones are little more than hand-held computers. So, it makes sense to be sure to optimize your site for mobile devices.

Optimizing means making your site responsive in terms of being easy and attractive to use on a mobile device.

Plus, your site needs to respond quickly to user clicks and swipes on mobile. A page load time of just 7 seconds can increase your bounce rates (people who leave) by over 30%.

Pro tip: You can check your site for free using Google page speed tool, Page Speed Insights.

## Make Your Blog More Professional

When it comes to the design of a blog, it should be clean, professional, and mobile-friendly. But, what else?

Let's take a look.

# Font

Use an easy-to-read font. Once you have found the one that works for you, you should be use it across all of your content.

Some good fonts are:

➢ New Times Romans

➢ Georgia

➢ Open Sans

➢ Verdana

➢ Roboto

➢ Arial

➢ Impact

# Clutter

Get rid of the clutter. While you might be looking to make your blog your primary source of income, a lot of inline ads, pop-ups and other flashy items are likely to put your reader off. When in doubt put them in the sidebar.

## Images

Use full-width images when you can. Beautifully written content filled with emotion or information will go to waste if your images are fixed width and small.

The flow of the material, in pretty much any content, will be much better when you use full-width images. It is much more aesthetically pleasing. Uniformity is beautiful.

Also, a good tip is to break up large blocks of text with your images. This will keep readers interested.

## Fold

You need to utilize the space above the fold. If you have a really large header, and then some adverts, you are forcing people to scroll down to read your content. It isn't always a bad thing but think about how often you scroll down on a site. I bet it isn't often. If you don't get a peek at what you need right away, you're clicking away.

Any content above the fold needs to be the hook, you need to tell people WHY they need to read the rest of the post. What does scrolling down give them? Nothing!

## Tests

The code for some themes changes, plugins change, and everything updates. If you aren't checking in on the content, you might find that people are having problems you weren't aware of.

When you perform a check use the menu to navigate through the blog, try scrolling down and see at what point your pop-ups arrive. All of this will benefit or inhibit your readers. The user experience is essential.

# Your #1 Tool is Clips

Let's talk about what you can put on that fantastically branded website. Before you can get hired, you need to prove you can write. But how can you prove you can write if you don't take free jobs to get a byline, right? Ah, that's the catch, isn't it?

I guarantee you already have plenty of great clips and if you don't they're easy to get. For example, anything you've written for previous employers, like website pages, brochures, newsletters, etc. is clip gold.

It doesn't matter if the piece has your byline. Your prospective clients understand that ghostwriting doesn't come with bylines and that most advertising stuff doesn't have bylines, either. They won't care that your name isn't at the top.

If you're just out of high school or college, dust off of those essays or reports that got an A and use the research as the basis for some awesome articles. If you were on the school newspaper and have some pieces you're proud of, those can be clips, too.

Have a blog? That sucker is chock-full of clips. Just go through and delete anything that isn't top-notch before presenting it to a potential client.

# Assignment: Gather Your Clips

Take screenshots or scan any copy you've written for previous employers' website, brochures, newsletters, etc.

If you have already dipped your toe into the freelance writing world, collect links to anything you have written for clients in the past. Remember, it doesn't matter if you have a byline or not.

If you don't have a blog, start one (on that great, branded website!) and post a couple pieces a day that are focused on your niche.

Keep going until you have a couple dozen strong, researched posts of at least 500 words. Remember to have a reader in mind and make the posts as interesting and fact-filled as you can. Don't forget to link to your references or cite them in your posts, either. This will make you look like a professional.

Write! Many places don't care if you're a published writer as long as you can write interesting, clean copy and have examples of your work. So, pick a topic that's within your niche and write.

Rinse and repeat until you have at least three really strong pieces. Once you're done, put each one in a Google Doc so you have links to send to potential clients. Be sure to lock the document so it can't be edited to protect the copy from being stolen.

# Put Together Your Portfolio

Now that you have clips, it's time to weave them into some awesomeness that potential clients will love. I suggest you make a portfolio using Contently and make another on LinkedIn.

Once they are up, both portfolios can bring you clients without the need to do anything else. I've had many people contact me for gigs because they found me on LinkedIn and if Contently likes your clips they may hire you to write for some of their clients. That's how I got a gig writing for Benefiber.

Bar none, I love Contently the most out of any online portfolio provider. It organizes your clips automatically, you can do automatic searches for clip using the platform and the whole thing just looks awesome. The best part is that it's free.

# Assignment: Build Your Portfolio (Separate from Your Website)

Create a portfolio through Contently by going to https://contently.com/register. Make sure you use your name as the portfolio's web address.

For example, mine is https://abradford.contently.com. This will help your portfolio pop up first when people google your name. It also just looks more professional.

Fill out everything in your account information, including your web address, if you have one, and your social media account information.

Every time you publish anything for a client, on your blog or on LinkedIn, be sure to add it to your Contently portfolio.

Once you have your Contently portfolio completed, head over to LinkedIn. Create an account and answer all the questions that LinkedIn asks to create your profile. Be sure to add any professional information that can make you look knowledgeable in your niche.

For example, if I decided my niche is health and I'm a registered nurse, you better believe I'm going to list my education and work history in that field!

Take a look at my LinkedIn profile to get some inspiration: https://www.linkedin.com/in/alin abradford

(And feel free to connect! I'll accept your connection!)

Now, remember those articles I told you to write in assignment #2? I want you to post them on LinkedIn using the publishing tool. To do this, click on the Home icon at the top of the screen and then click on Write an article.

Once posted, your articles can be seen by anyone who looks at your profile, plus you now have some more links you can add to your Contently portfolio. Look at you, getting all professional and stuff!

# Chapter 11: The Ultimate Guide to Finding Jobs as a Freelance Writer

Professional freelance writers are always blogging about these sweet gigs they're working on that pays $100 to $2,000 per article. Where the heck do you find these fantastic jobs everyone's talking about?

After years, I have honed a way to find great paying gigs quickly. Here are my secrets.

## Hit Up Social Media

One of the easiest ways to find gig gems is to search social media.

Often, businesses will post their need for a blogger, copywriter or ghostwriter on their pages. All you have to do is search for relevant hashtags.

# Assignment: Try Your Luck on Social Media

Put these hashtags into a Facebook or Twitter search bar to find awesome gigs:

#bloggerswanted

#writerswanted

#copywriterwanted

#bloggerjob

#bloggingjobs

#writtingjobs

#publishingjobs

#journalismjobs

#freelancewriterwanted

#remotewriterwanted

#fbloggerswanted (Fashion bloggers wanted)

#healthbloggerswanted

# Search Google the Smart Way

Searching for writing jobs on Google can bring up job posts from 2005 or jobs that are five states away and require on-site work. You can avoid all of the crappy job posts by searching smart.

If you want to search a certain site, put site: in front of the site name, then add keywords in quotation marks. For example, I've had a lot of luck with this search:

site:craigslist.org "remote writer "

Some other sites other than craigslist you can try are:

site:problogger

site:freelancewritinggigs.com

Some other terms you can try are:

"content writing companies"

"freelance writing companies"

To get newer job posts, add the date:

site:craigslist.org "remote writer "
July 15th 2021

Now the secret to finding high paying jobs: add the type of payment you're looking for.

site:craigslist.org "remote writer "
July 15th 2021 pays $220

site:craigslist.org "remote writer "
July 15th 2021 $50 per hour

site:craigslist.org "rcmote writer "
July 15th 2021 .50 per word

If you want to search everywhere, just leave off the site and type in the rest of the search. This will bring up high-paying gigs from company job boards that most people never look at.

**Hot Tip:**

Another way to quick search Google for gigs is to go to this link: https://bit.ly/2MI90M3

I set this search up for you. It finds all remote freelance writing gigs. Click on the Date Posted option in the menu to get the freshest posts.

# Assignment: Get Jobs Delivered to Your Inbox

Now that you know the search criteria, set up Google alerts so you can get these great jobs delivered right to your inbox every day.

To set up a Google Alert follow these directions:

1. Go to https://www.google.com/alerts

2. Type your search term into the box at the top of the screen

3. Click on the "Show Options" dropdown menu

4. Set it up to send you an email every day and to send you "all results"

5. Click "Create Alert"

# Sign Up to Get Daily Job Newsletters

There are some great sites out there that scour the web for freelance writing jobs, then bundles them up into daily emails. I've rounded up a selection that provides links to gigs that pay well. Here are my favorite daily and weekly newsletters you need to sign up for:

http://www.freelancewritinggigs.com

http://www.freelancewriting.com/newsletters/morning-coffee-freelance-writing-jobs.php

http://www.bloggerjobs.biz/

http://writersweekly.com/find-paying-markets

https://www.alinabradford.com/newsletter

# Assignment: Sign Up

Sign up to the above newsletters and check them for gigs every time they arrive in your inbox.

# Search LinkedIn

You have a fantastic LinkedIn page that you can use to show off your chops, but you can also use LinkedIn to find the best, most high-paying jobs. Click on the Jobs icon at the top of the screen. Then, in the search bar, type in (your niche) freelance writer.

Bada-boom!

You'll be presented with a smorgasbord of awesome jobs that pay well. You just need to find one that allows you to work from home.

On the same screen you'll find a "Job Alerts" option. Fill out the search criteria below the button, then click on it. Every time a company posts a new job that's a good fit for you, it will get delivered right to your inbox.

Here's a special way to search, too:

➤ Go to the Home page

➤ In the search bar type "looking for writer" or "looking for freelance writer"

➤ When it takes you to the page, click on the filter at the top of the page

➤ Choose the filter that shows the newest posts in the last week

Fresh posts by companies and individuals looking for writers will pop up.

# Pitch Magazines

Lately, one of the biggest questions I've gotten from new writers is how to pitch a magazine. For the modern freelance writer, the online world of published articles and opportunities to be featured in well-known magazines is daunting and intimidating. There's a right way to propose your pitch to the editor of a magazine – which means there's a wrong way, too.

There is so much competition out there for that spot to feature your article that it's worth taking the time to work out how to approach the big wigs and make a name for yourself. Here is a step-by-step guide to writing and pitching your article to a magazine.

## Research

Doing your research is paramount. You have to know the magazine you're pitching to reasonably well to know exactly how to address them. Read their latest publication and find out what kind of material they are most interested in. Then, read the last six issues. Really, get to know the style and type of article they like. I'm not kidding. Do the leg-work.

## Deciding on a Form of Contact

Once you've done your research and have familiarized yourself with the magazine, you need to work out whether to send an email or a letter. For the most part, email is best for this initial approach – it allows you to be brief in your proposal but clear in what you're trying to achieve. Editors don't have time to read an essay. If the magazine's guidelines require you to send a letter, though, do it.

# Getting the Contact Information

Finding the email address of the right section editor can be tricky. Here are some tips:

➤ Usually the magazine's website will have the information you need. Go to the contact page and look for the submission email address.

➤ If the site doesn't list one, go to the magazine's masthead (the listing of the people who work for the magazine usually found by the contents page) and see who the section editors are. Then, attempt to make contact with them through LinkedIn.

➤ You can also try finding out their email address by finding their social media pages on Facebook, Twitter or Instagram.

➤ Google the magazine's name and the words "submission guidelines." A little searching may turn up just what you need.

➤ Get a subscription to the Writer's Market. This site lists all the latest contact information. Or you can buy Writer's Market in book form if you don't want a subscription.

## How to Write Your Pitch

Begin your pitch with an eye-grabbing subject line that summarizes your story without going into too much detail about it. Then, start your email with a top-line in bold that summarizes your pitch. While you need to be clear with the context of your article, the editor wants to know what you want ASAP. Be specific and clear about what it is you're pitching.

What you follow up your top-line with is essential. You should include roughly 100 to 150 words of background to your title, allowing the editor to get a little more information about your article, without giving the whole thing away. You want to give them a taste of what you've written.

Finally, once you've filled out the email with your top-line and brief article summary, you want to finish off with a short bio about yourself – past work, achievements, why you want to write for their particular magazine. Keep it short and relative to their publication – only include information that reflects the kinds of things they're looking for in a writer.

# Follow up with the magazine

Once you've finished writing your pitch, don't just sit back and wait for the reply. Editors are busy people and have a lot of emails to get through every day, so part of the job is in your ballpark.

Once you've sent your email, wait three days and send them a follow-up, asking if they've received your pitch. Make sure to copy and paste the pitch into the follow-up email so that the editor doesn't need to go looking for it. I've gotten dozens of assignments just because I had the nerve to follow up with an editor.

It's a dog eat dog world out there for freelance writers pitching to magazines, and it's not getting any easier. You want to stand out from the crowd by producing an attention-grabbing, relatable pitch – it gives the editor the impression that you're seasoned and know what you're doing.

# Never Stop Searching

The key to finding gigs is volume. Apply for 20 solid gigs per week until you start bringing in the clients you need to pay the bills. Once you've got your clients, don't stop. You're never done searching when you're a freelance writer.

Start searching for clients that pay more to replace your current clients when the gigs end. Eventually, your name will get around and clients will search you out. That's how you know you've made it to the big time. Even then, don't stop searching. Just be super picky about who you take on as a client.

# You're Not Alone: Why People Will Pick You

Time for a pep talk.

You probably spend a lot of time dreaming about your writing business. You dream about how amazing it will be when you have tons of customers and you are making money hand over fist.

Then, you remind yourself: There is hundreds of others who have a business just like yours. The chance of your business beating out all the others is very unlikely. Then, you feel defeated and wonder why you are even bothering. You should just shutter your business and go to work for someone else. At least the paychecks would be steady.

I know! I've been there! Everyone who's ever set out to build their own freelancing business has felt that way, too.

Cheer up, buttercup. As long as you keep that attitude, your business will fail. So, every time you have negative, self-defeating thoughts, stop yourself. There are plenty of reasons why customer will choose you. You just need to be sure you're showing them why you're a great choice.

First of all, no one is you. No matter how many competitors you have, there isn't anyone who can offer exactly the same spirit, experience and ideas that you can.

For example, my profession is writing (duh). Many other writers have written for big name brands just like I have, but they probably haven't also worked as an editor, social media manager, photographer and illustrator. My unique experiences allow me to offer editing, social media and visual content services my competitors can't offer.

# Assignment: What Makes You You?

We've touched on this before, but let's go at it again. So, what makes you you?

Write down a list of what you can offer customers. Whenever you feel lost, refer to that list.

I keep repeating this assignment because it is vital to your success. You need to know what makes you special. You need to know your strengths and feel confident in presenting them.

# Chapter 12: Setting Your Rates

Choosing a rate is one of the most talked about subjects in the freelance writing community. There are many ways to figure out what to charge clients, but I'm going to show you how I do it.

# Assignment: Figure Out Your Living Wage

First, you need to decide on a living wage. This is how much money you need to make to get by in life. Go grab your notebook and write these totals down:

Go through your bills and add them up. This includes anything you make monthly payments on, like utilities, gym memberships, rent, car payments, insurance, daycare, etc. Include internet service, web hosting, etc.. that you need for your business in this category, too.

Now tally up how much you spend a month on gas for your car, coffee, groceries, clothes, haircuts and other things that you purchase each month. Include in this items you need monthly for your business, as well. Paper, pens, pencils, notebooks and the like all go in this category.

Add your bill total and your purchases total.

Most people forget to do this, but I think it is very important. Add $100 to your total for savings and another $100 to the total for fun stuff. Those are low, but you can increase your savings and your fun amount as you become more successful.

This total is your living wage per month. Every six month or so I calculate my living wage to make sure that I'm making enough to support my family and my business. If I'm not, I either adjust my rates or take on a new client.

# Assignment: Set Your Rate

Now that you have your living wage, you can set your rate. Take out your notebook again and figure out your rate using this method:

1. While writing articles, time how long it takes you to do each one. It takes me a solid hour to research and write an article that is around 500 words long, for example.

2. Take your living wage and divide it by 31. This will equal how much you need to make each day. So, if I need to make $5,000 a month my daily wage would be around $162.

3. Divide that number by the number of hours you want to work each day. This is your per hour rate. Okay, so if I work the standard 8-hour day and my daily wage is $162, then I would need to make $20.25 per hour.

It is important to note, though, that you won't be writing your entire work day. You'll be networking, brainstorming, etc. Plus, you won't be able to write one or two articles per hour for eight hours straight. Your brain will melt and you'll hate your life. So, take whatever you got for your per-hour wage and double it. This is your minimum rate for an article that would take you an hour to write. In this example, the article minimum rate would be $40.50. This is a super easy rate to make for beginners, by the way.

Once you have some clients and some nice clips, you can raise your rate and increase your savings and fun budget.

# When to Hold 'em and When to Fold 'em

Now that you have your rate, you need to know when to use it. You want to make the most possible, per gig, so there are some rules that help with that:

➢ Use your rate when looking for gigs. If a gig is offering less than your rate, give it a hard pass.

➢ Don't pass on a gig if it's offering above your rate. Shoot for the stars, baby! You can do it!

➢ Use your rate when a potential client asks what you charge.

➢ Don't divulge your rate when a client tells you their budget and it meets or beats your rate. Just say yes! Don't feel guilty. The extra will allow you to go above and beyond for your client.

# Chapter 13: How to Deal with Clients

Okay, you've gotten an email from a potential client. Do a little happy dance, then get down to business. Remember, confidence is key. My go-to reply to most potential client emails is:

*Hi (name),*

*Thank you for contacting me. Your project sounds like a great fit for me. What is your budget?*

*Thanks!*

Notice how I was quick and got right down to business. Don't feel like asking about their budget up-front is rude. If they don't want to tell you, then you probably don't want to work with them. These types of people end up screwing over freelancers. Trust me on this one. This approach weeds out the crappy clients and saves you a lot of time and heartache.

Now, when the client comes back with a budget that sounds promising, you can move on to more in-depth questions about the project. Another reason you ask about budget up-front is you don't want to waste time talking about their project if you'll need to decline when you find out they want to pay you $5 for a 3,000-word article.

I also avoid phone calls, for the most part. If they want a phone call, I say something like:

*I like to communicate through email or instant message so I have a written record of what we talked about. It's an important protection for us both.*

I'm not just messing with them for giggles. It really is a good idea to have a written account of everything discussed. This way, a client can't say, "Oh, well I told her on the phone I needed XYZ and she didn't deliver, so I'm not paying."

I had this one client tell PayPal that I didn't deliver what he asked for, so he wanted a refund. I sent

PayPal emails that proved I did everything he wanted. Guess what? PayPal sided with me.

Writing up a simple contract that outlines everything the client wants from you, the due dates and payment schedule is also a good idea. It doesn't need to be fancy. You can even copy and paste descriptions made in your emails directly into your contract.

When I work with big clients, they often have their own contracts written up, so that takes the burden off you.

# Dealing with the Jerk

As a freelancer, you're going to come across a lot of, well, just crappy people.

Here's one example.

I love helping clients, but nothing gets me more steamed than potential clients wasting my time.

This is one of my all time, number one time wasters. I was contacted by a man through email. He was very excited to get my help on his project, but things started off badly from the get-go.

First, he refused to look at my site to see what type of services I offer and wanted me to type it all out in an IM for him. Then, he told me that he had a budget of around $3,000. When I quoted him a price of $1,000 for my services, he changed his mind and told me that his budget was actually $400, but he could throw in an extra $100 if I could do the entire job. Plus, he wanted everything done ASAP and wanted an in-person meeting! Oh, and there's the charming fact that he said he wanted a local Texas writer, but wanted to pay Indian rates. Yes, he actually said that.

I told him what services I could provide him for $500 and that there would be no in-person meeting. I mean come on! There's no reason for an in-person when you can Skype. Besides, I'm not going to meet someone who randomly contacted me on the internet who has already lied to me.

After almost a solid week of him emailing me about how I need to help him and do his whole project ASAP, I got really fed up. I told him that instead of half up-front I required the total payment up-front. I mean if he's this big of a pain in the butt now, imagine what he'd be like during the project. After all of his emails, I didn't trust him to pay the other half, especially after he mentioned that several other writers disappointed him.

Here was his response:

*"Ok. Let's not start the work without any trust. If don't believe me, I don't need to believe your experience and trust.*

*Thanks knowing you and willingness to work with me.*

*All the best!"*

Well, let's see, dude. I have tons of references and screenshots on my site, proving my professionalism and I have tons of publishing credits. What do we know about you? That you are super unprofessional in your IMs and emails and expect someone with more than 18 years of experience to work for chicken scratch. I just can't get over his nerve.

You'll run into plenty of people like that, so here are some rules you need to incorporate into your business that will save you time and money.

Always make new clients pay at least half up-front. You wouldn't believe how many people have ended up not paying their bill for my services. Eventually, I wised up and put this policy in place. The only time I don't make clients pay up-front is when they are large, reputable businesses.

Use PayPal for payments. PayPal charges a small service fee and has a fantastic invoicing system. Plus, they can help you get your money if a client refuses to pay or they can help mediate if a client demands a refund. People give PayPal a bad rap, but you have no idea how many times they've helped me out of a jam. (And no, they aren't paying me to say that.)

Post your working hours on your site. I've had clients contact me at 2 in the morning over small stuff. If your working hours are posted on your site, you can gently point them out to any client trying to give you grief about not answering your phone during dinner.

Stay firm on your rates. Posting your rates on your site is your choice. Some writers do, some don't. No matter what you choose, do not haggle over your rate. If you haggle, then clients think you'll be lenient about other things, as well.

# Chapter 14: The Ultimate Social Media Toolkit: Templates, Cheats and Tips that Will Get You Noticed

After almost 20 years of creating content for businesses big and small, I've learned tips and tricks to grabbing a reader's attention. In social media, grabbing attention is essential to getting followers, likes, clicks and conversions. To your potential clients, someone who can leverage social media is a great asset.

So, I am going to share some of the quickest and easiest ways to peak readers' interest with you. Best of all? These are proven techniques that get results.

Anyhow, enjoy this toolkit!

# The Keys to Great Social Media Posts

There are several factors to creating a great social media post. These elements work no matter if you are using Facebook, Twitter, Pinterest or LinkedIn.

Photos are the most important element to any post. Short catchy text and hashtags are also important, but not as vital to engagement. (Except on Twitter and Instagram. Hashtags are EVERYTHING on Twitter and Instagram).

Here are some statistics that show the importance of each element to a social media post:

Tweets that are under 100 characters get 17% more

engagement, according to research by Quick Sprout.

Multiple photo posts increased clicks 1290%, according to a Facebook case study.

According to by Twitter, hashtags can increase engagement by 100%. You can go overboard with hashtags, though. When more than two hashtags are used in one post, engagement drops by an average of 17 percent.

Okay, you get the idea. Now that you know that using hashtags, photos and short text builds great social media posts, let's get to making those posts.

# Hashtag Cheat Sheet

For hashtags to be useful, people need to be looking for that phrase. So, you can't just randomly attach a # to just anything. Instead of looking up popular hashtags, I've made a cheat sheet to get you started.

The first seven are the "most liked" hashtags according to research by Dan Zarrella. The rest are hashtags that I have found get a lot of engagement.

To find the latest trending hashtags go to Hashtags.org. They list the most up-to-date hashtags by category on their homepage.

Remember, don't just add these all willy-nilly to your posts. Hashtags need to be relevant.

Here's a list of hashtags for you to reference:

1. #followforfollow

2. #likeforlike

3. #F4f

4. #followback

5. #tagsforlikes

6. #followme

7. #follow

8. #photooftheday

9. #picoftheday

10. #contentmarketing

11. #business

12. #smallbusiness

13. #socialmedia

14. #businessgoals

15. #retweet

16. #b2b

17. #sales

18. #blogging

19. #WP (WordPress)

20. #jobs

21. #love

22. #tbt (Throwback Thursday)

23. #me (This hashtag has bene used on 297 million posts on Instagram!)

24. #fun

25. #friends

26. #news

27. #android

28. #selfie

29. #lookoftheday or #outfitoftheday

30. Put a hashtag on any public figure or celebrity's name. For example, #Obama or #Beyonce.

31. #TGIF

32. #photography

33. #photobomb

34. #marketing

35. #beauty

36. #beautiful

37. #HappyNewYear

38. #Christmas

39. #ValentinesDay

40. #Easter

41. #IndependanceDay or add a hashtag to any upcoming holiday! You get the idea!

42. #android

43. #iPhone

44. #Apple

45. #app

46. #tech

47. #gemini

48. #capricorn

49. #libra

50. #aries

51. #scorpio

52. #virgo

53. #taurus

54. #cancer

55. #pisces

56. #leo

57. #sagittarius

58. #aquarius

59. #socialgood

60. #cause

61. #volunteer

62. #4change

63. #climate

64. #solar

65. #globalwarming

66. #drought

67. #edtech

68. #education

69. #teachers

70. #startup

71. #economy

72. #fashion

73. #health

74. #fail

75. #lifehacks

76. Add a hashtag to the name of an upcoming event like #SuperBowl or #ComicCon.

77. #backtoschool

78. Add "tips" to any other hashtag. For example, #healthtips, #businesstips or #fashiontips.

79. #art

80. #copywriting

# Social Media Photo Templates

You may have tried adding photos to your posts before...and, well, they ended up looking weird.
Why?
Because each site has their own image size requirements.

Here are templates you can follow to get the right look every time:

## Facebook

Images should be 1200 x 628 pixels for ads and 403 x 403 for shared photos. If you're uploading a PNG file, keep the file size below 1 MB. PNG files larger than 1 MB may appear pixelated, according to Facebook.

# Twitter

Photos can be up to 5 MB and animated GIFs can be up to 3 MB. 400 x 220 pixels is the best post size.

# Pinterest

Pinterest is the king of social media photo posting. For the best results, pins that are 600 x an infinite number of pixels look best.

# Instagram

Another photo king, Instagram has a particular post size that looks best, too. Make sure your image is 612 x 612 pixels.

All of this is summarized in the infographic, below. Feel free to share it on your site or social media accounts.

# Social Media Post Templates

Don't know what to say in your social media posts? Here are some ideas to get your creative juices flowing. These ideas are short and use emotion to grab the reader's attention:

1. (Fill in the blank) is the worst decision I've ever made. Here's how I fixed it. (Link to post or article.)
2. (Fill in the blank) doesn't look like this anymore! (Include a before photo and link to the after photo.)
3. Never make this (fill in the blank) mistake!
4. My ultimate (fill in the blank) list that will help you (Fill in the blank). (Link to your post or article.)
5. I'm (fill in the blank with something fun and silly) today. What are you up to?
6. I never (fill in the blank). Here's why you shouldn't, either. (Link to

your post or article.)

7. I never want to see (fill in the blank) again.

8. I finally (fill in the blank). This is why it took me so long. (Photo a photo or link.)

9. If you could change one thing about (fill in the blank with your business name), what would it be? (Get ready for honesty!)

10. Does anyone have a solution for (fill in the blank)?

11. Here's my new (fill in the blank). What do you think? (Selfie time! Post a photo of yourself with a new product, outfit, glasses...whatever you're following is into.)

12. Hold up! (Fill in the blank) is dangerous! (Add a link and a photo.)

# Automate Your Posts

Keeping up your social media accounts can be tedious, especially if you have several. I use automation to make it easy.

My favorite platform is Buffer. You can set up posts for several different social media accounts and schedule them to post at certain times.

Cost: Free

Works with: Twitter, Facebook, LinkedIn

Buffer's best feature is its Power Scheduler. This feature allows you to schedule a post to repost in a few hours, days or months on multiple accounts.

Another great feature is that by adding Buffer to your browser, you can craft posts from any account while you're using it. A Buffer button is added to the post screen.

After you press it, you can add a post to your schedule or add multiple posts, so there's no need to log onto your Buffer account in another tab.

Buffer also analyzes your posts to tell you which ones got engagement and which ones totally bombed.

# Assignment: Get Social

Set up official social media accounts for your new freelance writing business and invite people to your new accounts. You don't need to have an account on every single social media site. You can pick a couple favorites and go from there.

As your first post, announce your new business and share a link to your website. Then, brainstorm some posts and be sure to post:

➢ At least once a day on your Facebook page

- ➢ 2 to 3 times on Instagram

- ➢ 5 to 7 times a day on Twitter

- ➢ 2 to 3 times on Pinterest

Also, be sure to add me and I'll add you back. Here are my social media accounts:

https://twitter.com/alinabradford

https://www.facebook.com/nofluff writer

https://www.pinterest.com/alinab radford

http://instagram.com/nofluffwrite r

# Chapter 15: What Type of Writer are You?

Do I need a copywriter or a content writer? Is there a difference?

I've been asked this so many times. In fact, I just saw someone ask this question in a copywriting forum on Facebook. Some experienced writers don't even know the difference!

I've written articles about it for websites, but I thought I should probably lay down the knowledge here, too. Let's get started.

The difference between copywriting and content writing...in a nutshell

There's probably going to be arguments about this. Some people feel that content and copywriting are the same thing, but it really isn't in my opinion.

Here's the low-down:

Copy is marketing writing that does nothing but sell, like an ad or a marketing email. Content sells and/or informs or entertains.

Let's look at some examples.

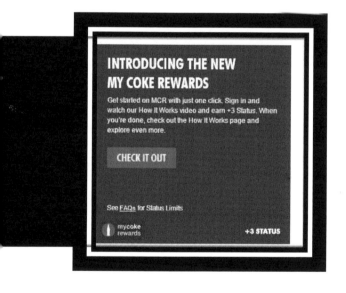

This example from the Coke Rewards website is simple copywriting. The whole goal of the text is to get visitors to sign up for Coke's new reward program so Coke can sell more soda. That's it.

The image on the next page is also presented by Coke. Its sole objective is to tell visitors about the mission and vision of the company. While its overall purpose is to convey a positive feeling about the Coca-Cola corporation, it also informative. A kid who is writing a school paper about Coke could go to this page and be supplied with facts about the company's mission. This makes the text content.

The world is changing all around us. To continue to thrive as a business over the next ten years and beyond, we must look ahead, understand the trends and forces that will shape our business in the future and move swiftly to prepare for what's to come. We must get ready for tomorrow today. That's what our 2020 Vision is all about. It creates a long-term destination for our business and provides us with a "Roadmap" for winning together with our bottling partners

## Our Mission

Our Roadmap starts with our mission, which is enduring. It declares our purpose as a company and serves as the standard against which we weigh our actions and decisions.

- To refresh the world...
- To inspire moments of optimism and happiness...
- To create value and make a difference.

## Our Vision

Our vision serves as the framework for our Roadmap and guides every aspect of our business by describing what we need to accomplish in order to continue achieving sustainable, quality growth.

- **People:** Be a great place to work where people are inspired to be the best they can be

What you're reading right now is content, by the way. If it was on a website, it would be considered content, too.

# Are You a Copywriter or a Content Writer?

You can take this quick test to decide whether are a copywriter or a content writer. Answer the questions by thinking about the type of thing you like to write most.

If you answer yes to these questions, you are a content writer:

➤ Does the text need to draw in traffic?

➤ Will the text be informative or used to engage the visitor?

➤ Will this text be shareable?

➤ If you answer yes to these questions, you are a copywriter:

➤ Is the intent of this text to sell?

- ➢ Will the content have a call-to-action?

- ➢ Will the content be used for direct mailings, sales emails, homepages or social media?

What if you need both? What if you need copy and content? Well, there are writers that do both types of writing very well. For example, I've written copy and content for big and small companies and they have been very happy with the results.

# What's the Difference Between Journalism and Content Writing?

There's one more type of writing I think I should talk about before I close out this chapter: journalism. Business owners tend to get news and content writing confused. A news article is one that excludes bias towards a business, product or person. So, if you are paying a writer to create a news article about your business to be published in a magazine or newspaper, that's unethical.

Think about this scenario:

A business owner contacts a journalist that writes for a print or online newspaper or magazine and asks if the writer would do an article about the business. The business promises to pay the writer for an article or a mention. The writer agrees and the article is published.

A totally legit transaction, right? NOPE. This is an incredibly shady practice.

A news article is defined as written content that excludes bias towards a business, product or person. If the writer is being paid by a business, there's no way the article isn't biased.

Most, if not all, news publications have rules about this sort of thing. As a writer, taking a payment is a great way to get fired and have your name smeared from here to eternity.

(For everyone about to blast me about big media: I'm not naive enough to think that money never exchanges hands in journalism, but that doesn't mean it's okay.)

If your business has a newsworthy story then you shouldn't have to pay for news coverage. A publication will want to cover your story. Plus, a publication writer is already getting paid from their publication. If they get paid by the business and the publication they're just double-dipping.

The exception to this rule is blogging. Independent bloggers don't get paid by a publication and may require payment to cover a business. This is called a sponsored post and if you take these assignments, just be sure to label the post as sponsored. In the US, you must label sponsored posts or you could be sued.

# Are You a Sex and the City Writer or a Dragnet Writer?

Your style of writing is important. It is what will make people follow your blogs and search for your guest posts. When you're deciding what your brand's voice will be, there is one thing you need to be clear on: Are you a Sex and the City writer or a Dragnet writer? Confused?

Let me explain.

# The Sex and the City Writers

Lovers of the iconic HBO series Sex and the City swooned at the thought of being Carrie, the main character. Carrie Bradshaw would sit at her laptop in her fantastic rent-controlled New York apartment, sip coffee or Cosmopolitans and type out juicy stories about sex and the Big Apple. Eventually, Carrie's fantastic stories earned her a spot at Vogue writing 500-word articles for $4 per word.

All of this is swoon-worthy, until you actually think about Carrie as a writer. She puts not only the most personal information about herself into her column, but she also writes about her friend's sex lives, her boyfriend's hang-ups and, once, about a politician's kinks. All of this is put out there every week for all of New York to read. She has no secrets, her friends have no secrets and everyone she runs into's secrets are often revealed, too.

This may seem far-fetched. No writer actually does that, right?

Actually, writers write like Carrie every single day. Some get paid like they are writing for Vogue and some get paid very little. They take some personal story or a story about someone they know and turn it into an article that gets right to the heartstrings of a reader.

Once upon a time, these types of writers called confession writers. Today, they are called bloggers or personal narrative writers.

Do you have the cajones to be a writer that delves into your personal life? Though I've dreamed of being Carrie more times than I care to admit, I just could never coax myself into the Carrie way of life. When sitting down to write a personal experience I would always wonder, "Will my mom read this? Or my kids?" Those thoughts put a stop to my more personal narratives. Maybe you don't have the same inhibitions, though. If not, you could create some amazing prose that others will love to read. And if they love to read your stories, they will keep coming back, gaining you site traffic and conversions.

# Dragnet Writers

If you have problems putting yourself in the spotlight you may be a Dragnet writer. For those that don't remember Dragnet from a time before CSI or never got a chance to watch some reruns, I'll give you the gist. The star of the show was Detective Sergeant Joe Friday. Friday was a laced up, no-nonsense type of guy who only concerned himself with the facts and how they pertained to his case. No funny business, you see.

While writing straightforward posts and articles may not be as flashy as steamy tell-alls, it allows you to get in there and present the facts to the reader in a quick one-two punch that gets the job done. The writer doesn't need to get sentimental or provocative or provide any personal information. If you like to present "Just the facts, ma'am," then writing the Dragnet way may be the path you take with your brand writing.

## Straddling the Fence

Of course, both of these types of writers are very drastic examples. There is a happy medium for those who don't want to lean too far in either direction. These writers pepper their fact-filled articles and blog posts with a personal story to add a little personality to their writing. This type of writing walks the fine line between confessional writing and news writing. You'll often see these types of articles on DIY sites, in home and style magazines and on sites like Huffington Post.

Don't know what type of writer you would like to be? Then you need to start writing to find out what writing style you are more comfortable with! It will probably take some time, but sooner or later your inner Carrie or Friday will emerge.

# Chapter 16: How I Write Articles for Big Companies

I make around $200 an hour writing articles and blog posts for websites. Want to know my process?

Here it is:

I Google my topic and read! I make sure to go to only reputable sites for my facts, though. Sites run by the government, universities, zoos and hospitals and the like are a-okay.

Next, I just write. Like, flat-out type. I get all of the facts out of my head and into a Word document.

Once everything is down, I divide it up into sections and order the sections in a way that makes sense.

I give each section a catchy (or informative) heading, then put it in

H2 heading format. (The format changes, depending on the site, but H2 is usually the go-to). Adding a heading format helps the article get found by search bots.

Now, it's time to back up what I say. I add quotes from experts (ProfNet is a great place to find experts) or I link to sites where I got the information. Links will also help your article rank in Google searches.

Finally, it's time for photos, videos, gifs or any other multimedia experience I can add. People are visual creatures and they love lots of things to look at. I add at least two.

Last, but not least, I go over the post a backwards and forwards to spot any typos, awkward sentences and other things that look totally unprofessional.

That's it. Once you have your process going, it's easy to create articles quickly. There's something to remember, though...

# Chapter 17: Dealing with Contracts

Now that you know how to write and find clients, you need to know how to deal with contracts.

# 5 Things You'll Find in Most Writing Contracts

When a client sends you a contract, there are going to be quite a few stipulations they're going to expect you to agree to. Let's look at some of the most common terms found in freelance writing contracts and examine how they will affect you in the long-run if you sign the contract.

*Note: I am not attorney, so please don't take this article as legal advice.

## Copyright

The copyright section (also called Assignment of Proceeds, Assignment of Inventions and Work for Hire) basically lays out who will own the work after it is accepted by the client.

There are several ways this section can play out:

➤ They want all rights, world-wide in digital and print, which means they own your work and you can't do anything with it after your client accepts it and pays for it.

> They only want digital rights, which means you can reprint your work in magazines, newspapers or books if you want.

> They only want US rights (or rights for whatever country), which means you can publish the work in other countries.

> They want print rights, which means you can publish the piece online, but you can't publish it in magazines, newspapers or books.

Here's an copyright excerpt from a contract I took on years ago:

*The Writer acknowledges and agrees that all of the results and proceeds of every kind of Work(s) rendered by the Writer for the Publisher—including, but not limited to: articles, stories, reports, memoranda, drawings, photographs, ideas, suggestions, titles, designs and other work— shall be, and hereby are, assigned to the Publisher. The Publisher shall have the perpetual and worldwide right, amongst all other rights of ownership, but not the obligation, to use and exploit the Work(s) throughout the universe in any manner whatsoever, in any and all media, now known or hereafter devised.*

Typically, freelance contracts will stipulate the company you are doing the work for owns all rights to the piece (as long as they pay for it). Keep an eye out for clients that allow you to keep certain rights, though. Keeping certain rights will allow you to earn money off of the work more than once.

For example, say the client only wants digital rights. You can go on and sell the piece to a magazine or put it in a book.

# Independent Contractor Status

This section basically states that you aren't employed by the client and that you work for yourself. By contract, a freelance worker or independent contractor:

➢ Is not covered by employment and labor laws

➢ Provides their own tools and work space to complete the job

➢ Invoices the company to be paid

➢ Pays their own taxes

➢ Is responsible for any legal actions that comes about due to misinformation or plagiarism in the work

It's also important to remember the legal definition of an independent contractor. According to Business Dictionary:

*To be legally designated as an independent contractor, an individual must (1) be free from the control of the client, (2) be able to exercise his or her judgment as to the manner and methods to accomplish the end-result, and (3) be responsible for the end-result only under the terms of the contract.*

So, if a company tries to get you to clock in, use only their computers or work only on-site, you are an employee, and the company is committing an illegal act by calling you an independent contractor.

# Confidentiality

The confidentiality section goes over what the client wants you to keep secret about their business. This can include trade secrets, how much money you make writing for them, their hiring process and more. Be sure to read this section and commit to memory what they don't want you to reveal.

Here's an example:

*You will not disclose nor use for your own or another's benefit, during or after the course of rendering services for the Program, any information not publicly known (hereinafter "Confidential Information) relating to the Company or any of its parent, affiliated or related companies, unless authorized in writing by the Company. Confidential Information shall include, but not be limited to, any information or data concerning any aspect of Producer's or*

*Company's operations or existing or future programming, or any other information regarding the Program; administrative and production procedures and manuals; business and financial plans, projections, results and prospects; computer programs and software; customer, employee, stockholder and supplier information or lists; Equal Employment Opportunity data, employee surveys, upward feed-back data, activities, plans; research efforts, trade secrets, Proprietary Property and technical information; trademarks under consideration; terms and conditions of the Company's contracts and agreements; as well as any information disclosed to the Company in confidence by third parties. You must preserve Confidential Information even after your services hereunder end.*

*You shall not make any statements to the press, any media service or other third party or distribute or circulate any written release, promotional literature, news story, advertising publicity or communications of any kind to any other party regarding the Company or any of its parent, affiliated or related companies, its programming services, operations and activities without prior written approval from the Producer or the Company.*

# Services and Compensation

The services and compensation section is my favorite. It lays down what your scope of work is and how much you'll get paid. Pay close attention. Some clients try to sneak extra work into this section that you didn't agree to initially. If you're not comfortable, don't be afraid to ask for changes.

Here's an example of this type of section:

*Our agreement includes:*

*Blog Posts*

*2 Weekly Blog Posts between 300 to 500 words on the topic areas of content marketing, native advertising and audience development, including the CTA.*

*1 or 2 Monthly LinkedIn Pulse Articles between 300 to 500 words on the topic areas of content marketing, native advertising and audience development. Articles will by posted to my LinkedIn Pulse under my name and will include a link or CTA to the Ideal Media site.*

*1 Monthly Guest Post around 500 words on the topic areas of content marketing, native advertising (though the word "advertising" will be used sparingly) and audience development. Finding guest posting arrangements will be worked on together.*

*10 to 11 articles, total.*

*XYZ Media will be invoiced $1,000 per month.*

*Social Media Services*

*Additionally, writer will leverage social audience, especially via Twitter and LinkedIn to promote these posts and the new blog site. Writer will also include any additional posts about the company needed. Included in this service will be the use of analytic tools to research the best times to post for the best engagement.*

*XYZ will be invoiced $500 per month.*

## Payment for Work

Here, your client will specify how soon you will be paid. Some will pay on delivery while others will stipulate a 15, 30 to 45 day time frame.

Here's an example:

*Writer, for authoring said Work(s), shall receive payment agreed upon for each article completed, submitted, and accepted by the Publisher. The Publisher will pay the Writer by check on 15th day of the following month for all Work submitted and approved by the Publisher. If the 15th occurs on a Saturday or Sunday, payment will be made the following business day.*

Be sure to check out the sample contract in the Appendix of this book.

# A Freelance Writer's Guide to Dealing with Digital Contracts

Say you land a new freelance writing client and they send you a digital contract. How do you sign it and send it back? I got this email from a No-Fluffer with similar concerns:

*Hi, Alina!*

*I'm one of your email subscribers and fans. I wanted to ask a question regarding freelance contracts:*

*How do these contracts work? I mean, how do you actually send them? Do I need a fax machine as a freelancer? When a client says I have to sign a contract, how exactly do I do that?*

*Full disclosure: I don't own a fax machine.*

*Thanks for reading!*

*Tara*

Those are all great questions, and I bet many other new writers want to know the answers, too. So, I decided to include a section on how to deal with digital contracts. Here's what you need to know.

## How You'll Receive a Contract

There are a few ways that clients will send you a contract. There's the DocuSign, PDF or a Word document.

The easiest way to deal with contracts is through DocuSign. Basically:

➢ Your client sends you a DocuSign link in an email

➢ You sign up for the site's free account

➢ The site will add the client's contract to your account automatically

➢ You sign everything digitally

Now, not all clients will be this easy. Typically, you'll get your contract as a PDF or Word document. This makes things much harder because you would need to print it out, sign it, scan it and then email it back.

## How to Skip the Steps

I hate the print, sign, scan process (mostly because my printer/scanner is always on the fritz), so I came up with a work-around.

If the contract is a PDF, there are two ways you can fill it out. Sometimes I take a screenshot of the page I need to sign, then use a photo editing app to add my signature and date. I keep a jpeg of my signature that I can place on any contract using the layering tool, then I use the text feature to add the date. To finish, I save the page as a jpeg and email the it to the client.

If you don't want to fool around with photo editing software, you can also use an online site called PDFEscape. It makes the document editable (meaning your can add your signature, dates, etc.) and it's free. Once you're done, the site lets you download a copy that you can email to your client. I used PDFEscape for one of my last freelance client contracts.

If you get a Word document, the process is much easier. You can use the insert tool on any word processor app (like Google Docs) to add your saved signature jpeg and then just type in the date. Save the document as a PDF and you're good to go.

# How to Create a Signature Jpeg

Okay, may be a little lost when I say I have a signature jpeg. It's literally just a photo of my signature. You can make a quick one of your own by writing your signature on a piece of white paper and then taking a photo of it with your phone.

Crop your signature image very closely so there isn't a lot of white space around the letters so it is easier to place on contract signature lines. Finish off by saving the image as a jpeg.

You can also open a new, white canvas using a drawing or photo editing app and write your signature using your finger or stylus on the touchscreen. Then, just crop and save it.


Email the image to yourself so you can download it onto your computer or laptop for whenever you need it.

Here's mine:

## What About Faxing?

Thankfully, most people don't ask you to fax anymore. If they do, you can always go to Office Depot or FedEx and they will fax your contract for a small fee.

# Chapter 18: A Freelance Writer's Guide to Invoicing

Freelance writing is a great line of work because it allows you freedom. The scary part comes when you start to look at your finances. When you take into account taxes, electric bills, internet fees and all the other things you need to run your work, the need for funds can mount up pretty quickly. This is why it's crucial you make sure your invoices always get paid on time by your clients.

It might take a while for you to get used to the thought of handling your own invoices and chasing up payments if they don't come on time. It's not as hard as it sounds, though. Here's my quick guide to help you out.

# What Needs to Be On an Invoice?

If you have never made your own invoice before, you're forgiven for thinking that you simply write down the price for the work and the clients details. It's not that easy!

Here are all the elements that need to be added on to the invoice to make sure you get paid:

➤ The clients order number if they have purchased a physical product.

➤ The name of the project or product which was purchased by the client

➤ Details about the work completed, including hours worked, if needed

➤ The total sum which needs to be paid to you by the client

➤ Your payment terms- add a payment deadline

➤ You bank details or Paypal info so that they can transfer you the money over

➤ Your client's name and address

➤ Your name and address

- ➢ Invoice number and date
- ➢ Registered business number and address
- ➢ Contact information

# How to Create an Invoice

Now that you know what should be on an invoice, how do you wrap it up into a professional looking package that screams 'pay me'? I like to use PayPal's invoice system when my clients agree to pay me through PayPal, but for checks or direct deposits, I use an invoice template I created in Word.

# How to Chase Up Your Invoice

When it comes to pursuing the payment of your invoices you might feel a little uncomfortable. Don't worry, it is totally normal for you to feel a little weird about demanding money from your client, but just bear in mind that you need the money to finance your business and your life. **Plus, you did the damn work, so you deserve it!**

If you have several freelance jobs going on at once, it would be helpful for you to create a calendar with reminders on when certain payments are due. (I use Google Calendar.) If the due date comes and the invoice has not been paid, you will need to contact your customer to find out what is going on.

It could be that they simply forgot, or they have another reason for not paying you. Send a gentle reminder and a copy of the invoice in an email.

If they ignore you, I've found that sometimes it helps to send a notice to a client's boss in the company to get things moving. For example, if you usually send your invoice to your editor, contact HR or the editor's boss.

# What to Do When a Client Won't Pay

If they refuse to pay, there are several things you can do. Pick the option that feels right to you:

- ➢ You can get the law involved since you sent them an invoice with a payment agreement on it. Send them a certified letter stating that you intend to take them to small claims court if they don't pay by a certain day. Typically, clients will get scared into action.

- ➢ You can open a payment dispute with PayPal if you sent the invoice through their services. All you need for proof is a screenshot of the email you used to send the finished article, blog post or whatever. A screenshot of the finished work on your client's website and a copy of your contract are also good things to send over to PayPal as proof of services rendered.

- ➢ Use the non-payment as a tax write-off. Be sure to contact your tax professional for more information on this option.

# Chapter 19: Here's the Legal Stuff You Need Before Becoming a Freelance Writer

You'll want to make sure that everything is legal before you go out and start to make money. Here's what US freelance writers need to start their business legally.

## A Name

Although you'll want to pick a name which suits you and the type of freelance writing business you want to start, you don't need to do this straight away. Use your own name. I've used my own name as a business name for 20 years. That's perfectly legal.

If you're dead set on starting off with a business name, you'll need to register it with the government before you can use it legally because it will become your "doing business as" (DBA) name. The US Small Business Administration lays out all of the rules for registering your small business on their site.

# Employer Identification number (EIN)

An EIN is the tax number that you will use to identify your business. You'll need it to work for clients, do your taxes and much more. Think of it as your business' Social Security Number.

# Business License

The last thing you will need is your business license. Many cities require that you have a license to own a business before you can start making money.

It will only take you a few minutes to fill out the form, and you will need to use your EIN to identify your business. To find out what licenses you'll need for your area, contact your local courthouse.

# You're Ready!

Congratulations!

If you've made it this far and completed all of the assignments, you've built yourself a solid freelance writing business. That's something to really proud of! Many people just dream of starting their own business, but you actually did it.

As long as your writing skills are good – and you continually work to improve them – sky's the limit. You can earn as much as you like.

Now, I offer you some free publicity. Tweet at me a link to your website, LinkedIn or Contently page and I'll share it with my followers. I'm @alinabradford.

Good luck!

**Need more? Join the No-fluff Facebook Group at:**

https://www.facebook.com/groups/440171039708533

Or search for **No-fluff Facebook Group**.

# Appendix

## Quick List of My 20 Favorite Sites for Free Media

- ➤ Giphy for GIFs
- ➤ Creative Commons for Creative Common photos
- ➤ YouTube for embeddable videos
- ➤ Easel.ly for infographics
- ➤ Meme Generator
- ➤ Pablo for quotes
- ➤ PhotoPin for Creative Commons photos
- ➤ DaFont for fonts
- ➤ Office Sway for presentations
- ➤ Pond5 for historic media files
- ➤ Survey Monkey for surveys
- ➤ NVD3 for charts

- ➢ Mapbox for maps
- ➢ OpenClipArt for clip art
- ➢ GetEmojis for emojis
- ➢ Pexels for modern, clean photos
- ➢ PhotoPin finds Creative Commons photos
- ➢ Pexel Videos for free stock videos
- ➢ ClipSafari for clipart
- ➢ MyEcoverMaker to create covers for ebooks
- ➢ Unsplash for free stock photos

# Reliable Websites to Use for Free, Credible Research and Citations

To find specific information on these sites google (topic) : (site name). For example, if I were looking for information about lions I would google lions : National Geographic.

> ➢ Profnet (to find experts for original quotes)
> ➢ US Food and Drug Administration (FDA)
> ➢ National Library of Health
> ➢ Centers for Disease Control and Prevention (CDC)
> ➢ World Health Organization (WHO)
> ➢ American Dental Association
> ➢ American Cancer Society

- The Journal of the American Medical Association (JAMA)
- Scientific American
- Mayo Clinic Online
- University websites
- Drugs.com
- American Academy of Pediatrics
- National Center for Biotechnology Information
- U.S. National Library of Medicine
- National Institute of Health
- Encyclopedia Britannica Online
- Geological Society of America
- U.S. Geological Survey
- The World Bank Open Data site (for world-wide demographic information)
- Merriam-Webster Dictionary Online
- Oxford Dictionary Online

- ➢ National Geographic Online
- ➢ ITIS (Animal classification site)
- ➢ International Union for Conservation of Nature and Natural Resources
- ➢ IUCN Red List of Threatened Species (endangered species list)
- ➢ National Science Foundation
- ➢ University of Michigan's Museum of Zoology
- ➢ Smithsonian National Museum of Natural History
- ➢ The Natural History Museum
- ➢ American Museum of Natural History
- ➢ Public Broadcasting Service (PBS)
- ➢ Fedstats and USA.gov (for US demographic information)

Pro tip: Need a specific scientific study for your research, but don't want to pay to access it through a scientific journal? Email the author or university that produced the paper and they will send you a free copy.

# Article Quality Checklist

- Does the title make sense?

- Is the title in the right style of capitalization for the publication? For example, are all the words capitalized? Or just this first?

- Does the title have good flow and include keywords?

- Take out the unnecessary "that" words found in your article.

- Check your "it's" and "its" to make sure they are correct.

- Are the headers in H3 or H2, depending on your client's requirements?

- Are there enough photos?

- Did you meet the word count requirement, if there is one?

- Take a look at all of the "an" and "a" words in your article. If they come before a word with a vowel, remember the it should be "an" not "a."

- Did you link to any sources or cite your sources correctly, depending on the needs of the client?

- Do all your sentences flow well? Remember to mix compound sentences and simple sentences throughout a paragraph to make the rhythm interesting.

- Make sure your paragraphs transition well.

- Are all of the sentences punctuated correctly?

- Cut any repetitions or unneeded words. (Remember, no fluff!)

- Does the overall theme fit the idea of the article, or did you go off track?

- Did you break down complicated steps into numbered lists?

- Did you make a group of items into bulleted lists for easy reading?

- If your article or blog has keywords, did you make sure to use them naturally, so they don't seem awkward?

- Is there a Call to Action or something to lead the reader to another page?

- Did you use first, second or third person throughout?

- Is the article or blog the right tone? Is it too formal or too casual, for example?

- Pretend you've never read this post before and know little about the subject. Is any of it confusing?

- Are there any videos or gifs you can embed to make the post more interesting?

- Did you include easy ways to follow you on social media though call-to-action or follow buttons?

290 | P a g e

# 30+ Sites that Offer Quick Freelance Writing Gigs

Now that you know how to write content you need to know of some places to look for gigs.

Here are more than 30 to check out.

Scripted: This is one of the best paying sites. Short posts are often go for around $50 after the site takes a cut. Some clients offer much more. They also work with big brands like eBay and StubHub.

Contently: This site gives writers free, awesome portfolios and often assigns high-paying gigs. One of my gigs there paid $360 per article.

DotWriter: You can get gigs on this site and also sell articles that you haven't placed elsewhere.

Textbroker: I'm not going to say this site pays really well, but there's lots of work.

Study.com: If you have a degree, you can teach classes and make some good money.

Article Document: I've heard good things about this site.

Blogmutt: This site has a lot of really easy, fast gigs.

Upwork: This is a site where you bid for gigs. Some writers love it, some hate it.

Studio D: The editors tend to be picky, but you can write for some big companies through this site.

Crowd Content: This site works with big companies like Best Buy.

BKA Content: You must be able to write 2,000 words a week to be a member of this site.

Internet Marketing Ninjas: No experience necessary to join this team. They will train you.

Zen Content: This company was bought by IZEA, a company I have worked with before.

Ebyline: Here is another IZEA property.

CrowdFlower: You complete simple tasks and get paid. It's a crowdsourcing site.

Express Writers: Great site for writers who know what content marketing means.

Editor Group: Accepts editors and writers.

Content Writers: 50% of every project payment goes to the writer.

Content Cavalry: They are looking for looking for specialists in business, automotive, content marketing, fashion, grooming, health, nutrition and fitness.

Writology: You can do client work and sell your own articles on this site.

ClearVoice: "Our ClearVoice platform matches clients' assignments with freelancers based on industry, pay rates and experience," the website notes.

Zerys: This site tends to have a lot of quick freelance gigs.

WriterAccess: Super easy place to make a few bucks.

Mediashower: They have, "Opportunities to advance to senior-level editorial positions."

CopyPress: Pay rates are $.04-$.06/word. Not great, but if the work is quick, you may make some cash.

Constant Content: "We currently work with brands like Sport Chek, Zulily, The Brick, CVS, Walgreens and more," they say on their website.

Pitchwhiz: A database full of the latest content calls from some of the biggest publications with the ability to send direct messages to the editors.

Listverse: Pays $100 per listicle (list-based article).

WordApp: I haven't tried this one, but I thought I would add it.

WittyPen: "On an average, the writers in Starter level are paid Rs 1/word. We pay flat pricing for each content piece you write with an average word limit," their website says.

Content Hourlies: The pay isn't close to great, but if you're fast it may be worth it...maybe...

Pitchwiz: Editors post their needs to the site and you can sort through to find websites or magazines that need your work. The dashboard offers you some gigs you may be interested in, or you can target certain niches and markets to create a custom search. There are really quality gigs at Pitchwiz.

# Where to Find Expert Quotes and Facts for Your Articles and Blog Posts

When you write a good article you need expert opinions and data to back up your topic. Where do you find all of
these knowledgeable people? Good question! Here is a quick list of places I go when I need information for my articles.


Profnet- I use this site the most. You type up a note about what type of person you need and Profnet sends it out to people that may be interested.

HARO- Help a Reporter Out is a lot like Profnet. The members are very closely knit, so you'll get help from other reporters, as well.

ExpertClick- You can find press releases, experts and news stories at this site.

TravMedia- Do you write travel pieces? Then this is the site you need to join.

NewsWise- NewsWise can send you the latest press releases and list of expert contacts to your email address. They specialize in health, science and life news.

Game Press- This is the go-to site for video game information. You can get contact information for gaming experts here, as well as news and press releases.

Association of Food Journalists- Foodie writers can find leads and information for food trend articles on this site.

Reporter Connection- I haven't used this site, but it looks like it works like Profnet.

MyBlogU- This is a collaboration site for bloggers.

Businesswire- Business writers will love this site. You can find press releases, market information and more.

Kiti- This site, formally Media Kitty, helps you "find unique story angles, news releases, connect with brands and network with media and influencers."

# No-Fluff Manifesto

**I am my own boss and
I don't take on crappy clients.**

**I am creative and
embrace my unique voice.**

**I get paid substantially
to do what I love.**

**I write amazing content
with no filler.**

**I am a No-Fluff writer.**

# Where to Find Me

Alinabradford.com

twitter.com/alinabradford

facebook.com/nofluffwriter

medium.com/@alinabradford

pinterest.com/alinabradford

instagram.com/nofluffwriter

linkedin.com/in/alinabradford


Don't forget to join the No-Fluff Freelance Writing Group on Facebook!

Made in the USA
Middletown, DE
05 January 2021